LESSONS FROM MY 20'S

Raven Martin

Lessons From My 20's

ISBN 978-1-7340368-3-1

Copyright © 2021 by Wilson-Rowdy Publishing, Inc.
Published by Wilson-Rowdy Publishing, Inc.
All Rights Reserved

All right reserved. No part of this publication may be reproduced in any form or by any means, including electronic, without mechanical or photocopying or stored in a retrieval system or transmitted without permission in written form to Wilson-Rowdy Publishing, Inc., except for brief passages to be included in reviews.

LESSONS FROM MY 20'S

Raven Martin

Dedication:

To every adult that ushered me into adulthood with what little guidance and nurturing they had. Your pour from what I now know was often an empty cup has made me a better human. I will forever pay it forward.

Foreword

Raven Martin is a gifted change agent. She uses her talent to encourage and empower people to move beyond their personal and professional limitations. As one of the nation's rising thought leaders, Raven takes a deep dive into the life of people in their twenties. This book is a must read for those who think they are going through a phase of life that either is challenging or carefree. This thought-provoking book will help you to manage and navigate your feelings and thoughts of your life as you experience and express your life.

-Dr. Leven "Chuck" Wilson

Reviews

Morgan Allison, M.Div., CPT - Our 20s are crazy, so I appreciate Raven pulling us "20 somethings" up with her. So many 20 somethings have been overlooked, misguided, misinformed, and misrepresented. It takes someone using real life experience from their 20's to understand the unique challenges modern 20 somethings face. Between student loans, existential crisis' around faith and relationships, we no longer need people looking down on us being dictatorial about what it takes to be successful. We need people like Raven who are in the position to help create policy change and impact real people's lives practically. She has a working understanding of the systemic issues we are facing and I'm certain her expertise will be something we can all learn from.

Kevin Sims, MS - Magnetic, Masterful, and Meticulous; This is how I would describe Raven as a human and as an author. Everything she speaks has purpose and promise which most naturally translates from ink to paper. If you aren't blessed to know her personally, reading her work is the next best thing.

Raven Martin

Sections

Responsibilities

Working Hard > Hardly Working

"I can't do anything I'm not passionate about"

My 20's Work Journey

Picking a Career

Relationships

Friends

Fun

Fickle

Forever

Love

The fundamentals

Take the Limits Off

Lessons From My 20's

Rose from the Concrete

Self

Who and what do you want to be really?

Commit to Kindness and Integrity

Trauma

Addicted to the story

Reality

Cry and Move

Spiritual Identity

There is More to You

Bad Religious Experiences

Fountain of Youth

Health and Wellness

Cheat Codes

Raven Martin

Responsibilities

The twentysomething era is hard. I know you're probably thinking like, duh captain obvious! I just feel it needed to be said even if just for validation and to affirm a young twentysomething going through this topsy turvy rollercoaster ride that is the 20's! It needed to be said in an effort to let them know that those feelings of uncertainty, fears of the future, constant pressures to level up, longing for fun and adventure while battling the need to be more disciplined and responsible, all of it, they're not uncommon. Whether you are in the budding years of your twenties and working out the kinks and wrinkles those teenage years leave behind, right on the cusp of thirty and scared out of your mind thinking how the heck did I get this old, or long out of your 20's and simply spending some reflection time during this life altering decade; the ride is just as bumpy and thrilling. Each year within this era is so riveting and many times feels existentially earth- shattering. Your brain is coming into its full self, your thoughts are becoming more abstract, and for most people during this phase, life is becoming more complex than it's ever been at any other phase in your life.

Lessons From My 20's

The weight of your world gets exponentially heavier, and decisions bare much weightier outcomes than they ever have. This on top of the fact that people are now in your ear so much more during this time, constantly asking about which direction you are going to head in regarding work, marriage, kids, and overall responsibilities. The killer part about the constant nag you hear about this, is that people say it as if you are not constantly wrestling with those thoughts in your mind already. Twentysomethings are often interrogated about their life decisions by people who, even though well meaning, leave them in places of heightened anxiety and frustration. The anxiety is due to an increasingly sensationalized and globalized world where we are forced to see constant images of what "a good life" is supposed to look like. But the irony is, the average twentysomething makes about 35,000 dollars a year and is constantly living on edge in so many ways. We *know* that "good life" isn't really a true reflection of our current lives. Those same images, coupled with this globalized ecosystem we now find ourselves a part of, makes us want to do and produce more. When we inevitably fall short, the feelings of failure and inability to level up settle in heavy. If I had a dollar for every time I've been confronted by a former high school classmate, a friend, or simply a random fellow twentysomething who shared with me their fears of failure I know I'd be rich. Fears of failure are a recurring theme in a twentysomething's mind even when at the peak, when you feel most invincible. This is because society hasn't provided a real framework on how to successfully navigate this age group. On one end we are told that you have time on your side and that your time should just be spent exploring and just going with the flow. Don't put too much pressure on yourself to figure it out because it'll all work out eventually is a common theme of advice. On the other end, you're constantly reminded about what things need to be done and made to feel foolishly naive about what hasn't been done or realized. This is coupled with pressures of their peers' journey sometimes making them feel as though they are somehow behind the curve of progress. The reality is that the truth lies somewhere in the middle of all those things. Wherever you find yourself while in that phase of life, you are right where you need to be because progress only requires a live and willing person to grab

Lessons From My 20's

hold to it. The only pressure that you need to put on yourself is the pressure to be better than you were the day before. In doing that, there are also intentional steps that must be made toward the right direction. There are things that absolutely should be done. There are certain relationships and decisions that should be approached with thought and intentionality. I found quickly that you cannot live your life directionless because it will have consequences later. So, the more seasoned adults that make you feel as though time is not on your side despite how much it feels like it during this time are right. There are a ton of things that you are not going to know about or fully understand unless you've walked through them, leaving much of your 20's up to trial, error, and evolution. This is where many of those same seasoned adults get their concept of approaching the 20's with a more free-spirited view. Because their lives often look completely contrary to anything they would have imagined while in their 20's, they counsel you to relieve yourself of some of the pressures---assuring it will all work out. Well, they are right too. The reason this sort of duality can exist between these two approaches to life is because there really is no cookie cutter way to find success as you journey into adulthood. I believe there are only universal truths and steps toward realizations that can be mastered to better position yourself to find the success that best suits your identity. What I have learned is that in making intentional steps towards my own future I've found more and more things about myself that I would have never imagined even a year ago. Those steps led me to depths of me that sparked interests and those interests' sparked passions, those passions sparked experiences, those experiences sparked relationships, and so on and so forth. The intentional steps towards something rather than the mindless abyss twentysomethings can easily fall into, led me into a purposeful abyss. And oh, an abyss it is! I do want to be very clear though, I am not romanticizing the process! It is my hope that this book does a good job in painting as real a picture as possible about the complexities of your 20's while also giving hope and optimism because there is absolutely room for it! What I've found is that there really is no nuanced advice given to this age group. There is often either all or nothing when it comes to the instructions given during this time. The advice is either a litany of words from already

Lessons From My 20's

established people that make it feel as though success is as simple as 123 or it's from a people who by all measured accounts failed in life and they have so many regrets that they want to protect you from a similar fate. It leaves you feeling like there is no strategy and no real way to plan, as though the only option is to jump out and just go, do, and be. That is the crux of what makes the 20's such a hard time, needing to be in a constant state of developing while not having a clue about how to actually develop. It has taken A LOT to get to where I am now. I'm only 27 at the time of writing this book, so I know there's a bit more to go but I've done a great deal of reading, crying, laughing, drinking, studying, eating, partying, counseling, and of course reflecting on and with the full range of people in this age group from all backgrounds. So, I'd say I'm pretty well-versed in all things twentysomething. Trust me, you can master this time. Now as we begin to journey into all the tips, thoughts, suggestions, zip zams and zoo doo's, I want to give you an outline of how I've dissected the 20's era so that way you can get a clear and concise understanding on how best to maneuver through it. The way I see it, your 20's experiences can be broken down into 3 facets, Responsibilities, Relationships, and Reality. Within those facets there are 4 rules of engagement that you MUST remember in order to thrive:

Rule #1- PAY YOUR DUES

Rule #2- CHILL OUT, IT'S THE FIRST

Rule #3- LIVE AND DREAM OUT LOUD

Rule #4- INDECISION IS STILL A DECISION

As you move along through the chapters, you must keep these four rules in mind! If you forget them don't worry, I'll be sure to remind you when a rule should be recalled and implemented, it'll just be your job to acknowledge and accept it. Now I will forewarn you, accepting them won't always be easy, you'll find that more and more as you move along through these chapters and are confronted with applying the rules in the necessary places in your life. But, if you stick along for the ride and are dedicated to yourself, I can assure you this decade will move a lot smoother for you if you're

Lessons From My 20's

new to it. If you find yourself reading this and you are out of your 20's, don't worry, I thought about you too. These tips, tricks, strategies, zip zams and zoo doo's can be universally applied. If you've found yourself feeling like you are a little behind the curve, just hop on board and remember there's no time like the present.

Raven Martin

Working Hard>Hardly Working

I don't know who started this fallacy of twentysomethings needing to be in the most invigorating career of their lives making at least 100K before they are even able to independently rent a car. Whoever it was tell them to call me because, in my most hood vernacular, "we gon' throw hands." This is such a large and dangerous lie that this generation has been sold and I have no doubt that it has contributed to much of the rise in nihilism and depression that has really taken root in millennials and Gen Zers. I need all twentysomethings to understand that in this decade, especially in the earlier years, it is not about loving your job or even being passionate about it, though that is nice. It is about making money and starting to stack the building blocks of what will be your identity. And to put it plainly, that takes hard work, both figuratively and literally. The quote "Rome wasn't built in a day" has never rang truer for a period in your life. With the rise of the internet and e-commerce, we have been able to connect with and see celebrities and millionaires in a way that previous generations could never have imagined. You can now capitalize financially off anything, including yourself. Because of this reality, we now have a completely romanticized view of what our 20's should and could potentially look like. Many have developed the mindset of, "If only it weren't for my piss poor job that consumes all my time with frivolous tasks, I would be able to frolic around like the internet stars on their trips and their daily exciting excursions." The problem with this expectation is that it misses the reality of the capitalistic economy in which we live. For your favorite internet star to live such a vastly adventurous life due to becoming famous from oftentimes nothing, there must be consumers who work in service jobs and other areas that aren't as popularized or glamorized. Simply stated there is a hierarchy of roles and, like every hierarchy, there's a thin margin at the top and a wide margin at the bottom. In all seriousness, the likelihood of you obtaining that same lifestyle or even one slightly close to it is slim to none, especially not this soon. I am not trying to quell your dreams and aspirations, its actually the complete opposite. I am here to tell you what a lot of mainstream information sources do not, that to be successful at life requires hard work. Full stop! There is no room for if, ands or buts. The few that get lucky and get to forgo hard work in the traditional sense are sheer reflections of just that, luck. Now I am not saying that many of the internet stars don't do a lot to get and maintain where they are. As a person who's been working to develop a platform worthy of attention and one that people frequent, I know firsthand that it takes a lot of hard work and long-term commitment, especially to monetize it long-term. Other times, however, the level of success that many of the internet stars have reached is oftentimes the result of a viral video clip that they've used to capitalize from and grow their following. There is absolutely nothing wrong with this and as you read further, you'll find that I am a staunch proponent of capitalizing on your gifts. However, this generation of quick wealth builders has not come without its consequences on our culture and how we view success. The frustrating part about our desire to all become the next big internet sensation, or at least live the lifestyle of one before the age of 25, is that the glorification and borderline obsession of this glamorized and overindulgent lifestyle almost simultaneously glorifies the lack of a strong work ethic---and I can assure you that

Lessons From My 20's

is dangerous! Now, before you get all mad at me and call me an old "bitter betty" who doesn't understand, let me explain. When you see these glamorized lifestyles on the internet, they often don't tell the whole story, thus giving you a fraction of the picture and leaving you with a piece of an image that leaves you feeling as though your life is not as good. It has the tendency to leave many feeling like they are missing some pieces, and that they haven't been able to attain relative success because of it. So even if that internet personality has or has not worked particularly hard for their status, you as the consumer would never really know because people post the finished product. In your mind you are now left with feelings of lack and that you are again somehow behind the curve of success.

The irony of this generation's intoxication with becoming the next big overnight hit is that most people that live lavish lifestyles are either profiting from people in the past who worked hard for that money or have themselves got it out the mud and developed wealth. The quick overnight millionaire or millionaire internet star is not even closely representative of the average wealthy person in this country. Most people don't begin to develop real wealth until their 40's. I know that just burst a lot of people's bubbles, so take a seat and breathe deeply if you have to. Look at some of the household names that we all follow and cherish in our culture. Joe Rogan, Amanda Seales, Charlamagne the God, Angela Rye, and so many other tv hosts, entertainers, and thought leaders that have made a lasting and substantive effect on culture are often all over 40. Note I said lasting and substantive. I know that there are a ton of YouTube stars and Instagram influencers who are famous for reaction videos, pranks, and shock jock culture, but the reason there are so many is because they are constantly popping up. The lane is over saturated and has a high turnover rate. Each person is always at risk of the next person booting them out by doing something even more ridiculous than the last. Even if we step outside of the entertainment industry and look at any notable doctor, lawyer, or general professional, they do not begin to acquire real wealth and influence until well into their careers. Entrepreneurs are the same, all the studies show that you must be in business for at least five years before you even begin to see any real profit. Many hope to just break even in those first two to three years. This is

Lessons From My 20's

because money compounds. It compounds not just by acquiring it but also by relationships, proximity to it, experience, and information. If you have not been making money and developing substantive relationships and experiences for 90% of your life, it's foolish to think you will just walk into a boatload of wealth haphazardly in the last 10%. You make money, you then move money, and you continue to make more. You develop relationships, you work those relationships, you evolve to places with more money. You go through experiences, you grow, learn and become wiser, and you move smarter and attain more wealth. Simply put, as people move through life, they continue to make more money, allowing it to compound. So, this pressure that so many twentysomethings feel to be like the wealthy people they see reflected in media and elsewhere, is really misplaced. If not put in the right context, you set yourself up for failure and disappointment in comparison. The day that I stopped living off the financial standard that my 16-year-old self set for my 20's was the day I truly started living, enjoying, and making the most of my financial profile at that time. I did this by saving what little I could with the jobs that I had. I spent probably a little more than I should've but still stayed within the limits of what I was making at the time. I was intentional about making sure my responsibilities were in order first before participating in recreational activities. Most importantly, I recognized that I wanted to increase my earning potential which led to setting realistic goals for myself rather than comparing myself to already wealthy people, internet stars, and other naive expectations I had as a child. Neither of those realities considered the complexities of adulthood and what it takes to acquire lots of wealth or to build a financial identity that is both fulfilling and worthwhile.

So, with that, the message is simple, don't fret humbler beginnings. We have been sold this notion that you can skip the grind phase and move right to happily ever after. Money, status, fulfillment, and purpose seems so easily accessible nowadays, making the hard work that it requires to flesh out a whole person who is emotionally and mentally well-adjusted enough to even have loads of wealth, look like a cake walk. It's not! Furthermore, the reality is, everyone is not going to be a millionaire or even wealthy

Lessons From My 20's

(in the monetary sense) and that is ok! But, on your way to whatever status of wealth and success you will attain, it is so critical that you remember it is not going to happen after you watch one YouTube video on wealth and entrepreneurship or read one article about how to become a millionaire in five short steps. Even if you were one of the few .000001% of people who happen to stumble upon great wealth and success early, your capacity to maintain and handle all that it encompasses effectively is increasingly slimmer because of the simple fact that you have not had enough time to even carve out your identity and value system yet. There is a reason why child stars and young rappers are always in the news with some sort of scandal or report of reckless behavior. There are critical cognitive, social, and emotional skills that must be developed prior to being thrust into massive amounts of wealth and exposure. Now before you roll your eyes at me and dismiss what I am saying as old fashioned and misguided, please know I am fully aware that our generation despises older people lecturing them about how much they do not work hard and commit to work. I also know full well the economic disaster the millennial and Gen Z generations inherited. Still, those older sentiments previous generations shared have never felt more relevant to me until I started to see the benefits of paying my dues in my work life and working for my progress. We all know what happens when older people are expressing their disdain for our work ethic, they start with a story of how much work and effort they had to put into that crappy job they had when they were our age. When I was younger, I would find myself being rather dismissive of those stories because I thought to myself, it is a new day and we thankfully do not have to endure the same struggles as previous generations. Though that is the truth regarding things like workplace conditions and even work options, the principles, and philosophies they were sharing will always hold true and relevant. Things like, "proper preparation prevents piss poor performance" (S/O Laurence Ray) will never die and will always remain applicable! Go get it out the mud, maintaining as positive a disposition as you can, and enjoy the beauty of small beginnings. Build relationships at work, laugh, and remember these days with pride so you can yourself be an older

Lessons From My 20's

person one day who can tell a twentysomething "I worked hard for EVERYTHING I HAVE!"

Raven Martin

"I can't do anything I'm not passionate about"

I don't know about you, but I need money to survive! You can't live in this world without money and last I checked the only way to get money is to provide a service or a good to either an employer or to people. AND THAT IS OK! If you are not passionate about your job and you're in your early 20's, you're right where you need to be. Your beginning and mid 20's is about learning who you are, finding what you're passionate about, and learning to navigate the world as an independent adult. The first rule to true independence is making it happen at all costs and working your way there. Again, I cannot stress enough that this is not an overnight process. I know people like to talk tough grind culture on social media but really aren't about that life of making it happen no matter what. "Started from the bottom now we here" is not just catchy Drake phraseology, it's a mantra that has to be executed. Passions must be afforded. You don't like where you work right now? Cool. What steps are you taking now to make sure you won't always be there? Are you taking steps or making excuses? Quitting that job you hate prematurely is not always the option.

Lessons From My 20's

Sometimes you have to stick it out while you formulate an exit strategy. And I don't care what anyone tells you, don't exit if you don't have an entry into something else! I know there are promising stories of those who do this and see success but those are few and far between. Why do that when there are so many more seamless and less painful routes to your dreams? You always need to be employed while working towards something because you need money. Again, money compounds so essentially money makes money. So, if you are wanting to do more and have more access to things and rooms that will get you more money, you have to first have some. You must then learn how to manage and maintain money at the level that you are earning it. If you are incapable of making responsible decisions with the money that you are earning at this stage of life and at this job, then you can't just expect yourself to know how to properly manage more wealth as it comes to you. This is a principle that can be universally applied, mastering where you are will help you develop the discipline to move forward to more. Starter struggle jobs are the name of the game. For everyone super wealthy twentysomething social media influencer or entrepreneur, there are 1,000 broke ones checking their account to see if they can afford that Subway sandwich at lunch. That is just the name of the game. I know we like to think of ourselves as the "different" one and that we are going to be the ones that break the mold. We tell ourselves in our early 20's, "Not me! I don't have to do that dead end stuff. I can chase my passions." To that I say, yes dear you can, but even passions cost. And they do not just cost money. They cost discipline. They cost perseverance. They cost steadfastness and vision. They cost character and morale. These are developed and strengthened in times of hard work and effort given in places that you may not like but that still profit you something. Whether you like it or not, while working in jobs that you are not necessarily passionate about, you are getting a paycheck that is providing you with money to pay your bills and to eat. Believe it or not, a warm bed and food on your plate makes it a heck of a lot easier to actualize your future dreams and chase your passions. If you're living at home with your parents and they are still providing you with the necessities of life then great, but that doesn't negate your need to take seriously your need

Lessons From My 20's

to work and work hard. You too must know that this free ride won't last always and even if it possibly could, do you really want to be living on your parents' dime for the rest of your life? What will that do to your self-esteem? What do you want to contribute to the world? Whatever those answers are I can assure you the route to them is through the vehicle of hard work and progress during the process. As I am saying this, please do not hear what I am saying as an invitation to accept anything less than what you are worth. You are a bright beautiful and talented human being with a world of opportunities within you waiting to be manifested, and I mean that; but you need discipline. You need a plan. You need focus. You need to master the art of sacrifice and compromise for something greater. That vision you have on the inside of you that you want to come to fruition can only happen with the expanded version of yourself. Contrary to popular belief that expansion does not happen at the top, it happens in the trenches. I've found that the phrase "choose a job you love, and you will never have to work a day in your life," needs to be completely thrown away. Work is an inevitable part of life and this quote, well-intentioned as it may be, has sold us a fallacy of what our day-to-day life should look like. Life is a mixture of work, play, and leisure. This is not to suggest that work should be strenuous and taxing all your life, because there is no reason you can't love your work. However, when presented in a way that suggests that if you love it then it won't feel like work, it's leading people on a fictional journey and it's dangerous. Loving a job does not mean that it will not sometimes be taxing on you. The beauty of working hard is that it gives way to fulfillment and strengthens our core values and self-esteem. We must as a society move away from this notion that hard work and things that produce difficulty are things that should be avoided. History bears out the weight of this truth, anything noteworthy and lasting must be fleshed out and earned. So, here is my advice to you on how to make that job that you perhaps hate and this interim time in your life the most fruitful it can be: Show up to work every day with a can-do attitude and give it 100% and create habits that reflect the life you want to live. What you give to the places that mean the least to you speaks volumes about who you are and who you want to be. There are always going to be things in your life that

Lessons From My 20's

you dislike and even completely abhor, but the art of "adulting" is learning to master your surroundings and making the most of everyday. You are not giving your all to the company for the company's sake, but for yours. If you do not develop a strong work ethic now, it's not going to magically come if and when you finally get to do what you want to do professionally. The work ethic and skills you need to develop are lying within the small details of your everyday life. Yes, including that job you hate right now. Find something to glean from your current workplace and if nothing else, leave a positive and lasting impression on the people there because you never know who you will need one day and what your life and work ethic could mean to someone or somewhere. In time you will see more and more how valuable your impact in places and on people really is.

Raven Martin

My 20's Work Journey

When I was 18, I went off to school in Jackson, Tennessee and had an amazing time and met amazing people that I love and cherish to this day. Then I came home for my boyfriend at the time, leaving behind all that I knew and loved because I loved him and wanted to be with him (*eye roll… we'll stick a pin here and revisit later.) My short-lived time at my historically Black college was wonderful and l loved every minute of it and some days I regret deeply not staying there. I instead came home and enrolled in a small Christian college that most people would not be able to find on a map. Fast forward three years and I graduate from there with my bachelor's degree and obtain my first real grown-up job at a local community mental health agency. You couldn't have paid younger me to believe that I was not going to be graduating from an HBCU and on my way to law school, but in real 20's fashion you can have one vision for yourself, and life will take you in a completely different direction. By the time graduation rolled around I figured that I would just attend graduate school and get a job in my field. I did not have a real plan other than knowing that I

Lessons From My 20's

didn't want to be a failure in life, so I had to pursue something. This is an important point to make note of so if you're taking notes, write this down: There is a happy medium between knowing exactly what you want to do and going after it, and not knowing and living the bulk of your 20's aimlessly. That medium is what Dr. Brittany Conners calls *Failing Forward*. Failing forward basically means that if you are going to fail or get deterred, the least you can do is fall in a forward moving direction. I knew that I did not want to work in some of the service and retail jobs that I'd worked while in school and I also knew that in order to get to the places I wanted to be I needed money, experience, and a worthwhile resume. So, while moseying along just figuring it all out, I continued moving in a forward direction. Along the way I would say that I would be going to law school, I would be a teacher, I was going to run a nonprofit, and that I was going to run for political office. These are just a few of the things I had asserted I'd be doing by now. While uncertain, I worked. While confused, I studied and explored. I learned what it took to be a lawyer and started studying for the LSAT but once I figured out that I wanted to be a lawyer for selfish reasons, I opted out. I started a few nonprofits that fell through because I had to fine tune my passion and as I've gotten older, I've been able to narrow it more and more to what it is now. During college I worked in afterschool programs and did an internship at an inner-city elementary school and realized that wasn't for me either. While working my first full-time grown-up job out of college, I met a woman in my office who was running for congress. I began working with her to help her get elected. That time on the campaign trail really invigorated me and solidified my love and passion for policy and politics that I had only recently realized and developed due to a horrible breakup with the same guy I came home for, (whew chile). All these presumed failures and detours were shaping my worldview and giving me real work and world experience that has helped me to come to this more specific view of what I want to do. And boy am I excited about my plan now! What those earlier years in my 20's taught me is that this decade of life really is inevitably chaotic. That said, you can bring organization to them. Before we can even begin exploring your professional identity and what type of worker you want and should be, you must

Lessons From My 20's

first understand that in your twenties it is your job to un-muddy the waters you are beginning to wade through. What that looks like is establishing some order in this decade of firsts. I had to get out there and take risks, do the not so fun stuff, network and break out of my comfort zone to make sure I could expand. I learned, you must be prepared to make choices, sacrifices, and compromises to get to a desired destination. Expanding your worldview and perspective will help you navigate this decade more peacefully and with less disappointment. I'd be lying if I said that I had it all together or that I will ever have it all together. Work some days is challenging and planning for my future is a taxing process that sometimes gets the best of me emotionally. That said, I realize that it is not necessarily about having it all together especially in terms of my work and professional goals, but rather the continued growth along the way. I have been fine tuning my skills and my abilities over the course of my professional journey and each of my positions have shaped my intellect and capabilities in invaluable ways.

Picking a Career

Let's refer to our handy dandy rules here. For this section we will be working from the following rule:

Rule #2: Chill, it's the First!

The running advice that all twentysomethings get is that time is on your side and that you have all the time in the world to pick a career. That is neither wrong nor right advice, it just requires context. This is the only decade where you are framing an adult life out of nothing but the shards of childhood. Most twentysomethings are coming out of complete or partial dependence on a parent or guardian and entering a setting where they are now solely responsible for their well-being. Picking a career at this time is rather difficult because again, you are choosing with tools that have yet to be fully developed. Your likes, interests, passions, etc. are useful in picking a career, so it is vitally important that you cultivate those things during this phase. I empathize completely with the argument that you have time to figure it out

Lessons From My 20's

because truly you're not going to know yourself for a while. Now is the time to just buckle up for the drive and chill because it's your first go at it! Some of the confusion that you experience during this time is actually good and should be embraced because it is evidence that you are being thrust into a big, beautiful world loaded with opportunities that are at your disposal. You can legitimately do anything! I know that there are a lot of nuances that come with that statement, so I do not say it lightly. Many times, opportunities are dependent upon certain levels of privilege one has been born into. To many, the statement you can legit do anything is often seen as another privilege and something only a privileged person would say. I get it! But to that I still say, you can legit do anything. The world is your oyster, even if the opportunities placed in front of you are slim to none and your road to a successful career in whatever you so choose is a bit rockier than a person born into great wealth and opportunity. There is still an avenue for you to get wherever you want to go, even if you must carve it out for yourself. The question simply becomes, how bad do you want it? How disciplined can you really become to attain it? If the answers to either of those questions are even slightly uncertain then you still have some self-work to do but we'll get there later. For now, let's talk about what it will look like picking once you've made your commitment to be your best self and achieve everything that you set your heart out to do. The number one piece of advice I give to all people trying to find a field of interest that they are willing to do every day is largely tied up in rule #3, **Live and Dream Out Loud**. What that simply means is you must dive into life all hands-on deck and be willing to take actionable steps towards finding a path that is right for you. I know that is not the rosiest of answers, especially because it seems vague and cartoonishly optimistic but that really is the only way. There are a ton of different career aptitude tests online that will help point you in the right direction of finding the best professional route to take. To live and to dream out loud means that your desired career and overall position in life has to be one that exists outside of your dreams at night. It must develop a life outside of your conversations with your friends and those you are most close with about what you've "always wanted to do."

Lessons From My 20's

If you have always thought about owning a pizza shop and everybody on the block has always praised you about your pizzas, don't get angry that you don't have one yet, this is the perfect time to start evaluating what it will take to get one. What does it look like to run a pizza shop beyond the clout that it would provide you on social media? How many boxes, how much dough, what's the best area, who's the top selling pizza shop owner near the area you like the most? The dream is in the head, but the success is in the rest of the body doing the physical work required to fulfill it. It literally does not matter how much you talk about it or how much people rave about how good your pizza is if you abstain from taking actionable steps to obtain it. If you feel as though this pizza shop is your dream, while you wait in the interim stacking money and doing your studying to be most successful, you should also be finding people in that industry to help get you there. Since you must work during that time to make it, why not try and find a local pizza shop that is hiring for a driver or a cook and master all you can while you stack and study? When you make intentional steps like that towards your future, those interim days become less and less stressful and frustrating. You are working toward an expected end while also learning and financially supporting yourself. You are living and dreaming out loud, putting hands and feet to a dream in your head. Dreams are costly, and you pay for them every day you put in the work to bring them to reality in both the big and small tasks. Now, if you are someone who has not really found their niche yet and you have not been dreaming about what you want to be doing for years, that's ok too. Dreams don't always come readily available like that. As long as there is breath in your body there is time, the type of time just looks increasingly different as years go by and responsibilities thicken. Just remember, you have never seen anything evolve from nothing. Things evolve from something already established and you cannot establish something by doing nothing. If you are not careful the pressures to pick a career path so quickly can also paralyze you, because the process is scary. The fear that you feel should be exciting because you are about to embark on an entirely new phase in your life that will largely be an added archive and will shape your future. Remember this is only the first phase of your adult life so

Lessons From My 20's

don't feel frustrated or angry at the notion of having to pick something. I can assure you; life is going to throw you so many more choices and opportunities that this choice will just be practice. The benefit of choosing a solid career path now is that you save yourself the heartache that perpetual uncertainty brings. All the research bares out that young adults who have made a choice and are on a specific path feel much happier and more optimistic about the future than those who are perpetually on the path of indecision. To be confused about which path to take is not the same as being indecisive about a path. At some point you must weigh your options and pick the one most suited to your liking. Life does not stop moving forward and you do not want to wake up and find yourself in a cyclical idea loop because you were too afraid or lazy to make a choice and put in the work required behind that choice. When trying to figure out career paths I challenge all twentysomethings to have a self-reflective conversation about who they are and what they want out of their lives. Let's take a moment, reflect, and ask yourself these questions.

"What am I currently passionate about that aligns with my overall self?"

Yes, passions vary but some passions we have are integral to who we are as people and can be used to make some identifications about ourselves. So, start there and choose the one that is most important to you.

What are my interests thus far?

Again, interests may vary as well, but at this juncture in your life what are you most interested in that you can see yourself pursuing. The reality is that what you feed is what will grow. As you pursue it, the chances of it expanding into something that you outright love and enjoy doing is much greater than your chances of success not doing anything because of indecision. These are the types of questions that must be answered when seeking what career paths to take in your 20's. In my experience, I have found that many twentysomethings try to avoid the more concrete approach to these questions. Usually, they would much rather leave their answers to these questions in the abstract because it allows them to

Lessons From My 20's

forfeit responsibility for a little while longer. The impression that I have always gotten is that it makes them feel better about themselves to be able to hold on to the "I'm still figuring it out" moniker. But if you have not heard let me be the first to say to you, indecision is just a product of fear; fear of the unknown, fear of failure, and frankly fear of growing up. So no, do not be consumed by the pressure to pick a career path so much that it cripples you into indecision, but you also can't avoid it either because life is going to go on whether you decide or not. It comes down to simple realizations, would you rather be the young person with some money in their pocket and a solid foundation you've built for the future, or the one heading to your 30's without anything to stand on because you neglected to choose a path? What often happens when choosing careers is that twentysomething's work from the mindset of their childhood self because that is the self that they have known the longest. Think for a second about how children approach hard decisions. They usually report to the adult in the room or simply avoid it altogether. You mustn't look at career options with this idealist and childlike lens because the difference is, there is no one to report to but yourself this time. Look at choosing through the lens that reminds you that something has to be done because you need money to survive and to thrive as well. I encourage many of my peers and clients to begin shifting their lens from what success is from their childhood view to the view that honors who they are becoming. It is imperative that young adults are able to approach their career choice with a mindset of contentment and fulfillment rather than being caught in the loop of indecision and apathy. I promise not making a choice will leave you so much more disappointed with yourself in the long run. I am not asking you to be complacent with a decision but rather reach a place of contentment, and there is a difference. Complacency says, I am going to be stuck here forever so there is no need to try to do anything else for work. Contentment says, this is where I am right now so I will give it my all, be grateful for the life that it is affording me and continue to work and progress. You may not be doing the most glamorous of things or substantially changing the world in record breaking ways right now, but when I encourage my twentysomethings to complete this exercise, I always make sure

Lessons From My 20's

that they are doing it through the lens of their newly found adult self. That adult self is who must show up every day to produce results and build a life that honors that beautiful child self that lives within them.

Raven Martin

Friends

Research shows that friendships in your 20's get more serious and longer lasting. This is because life begins to require so much more from you and responsibilities thicken. During this stage, many are finding life partners, having children, establishing careers, and creating an overall life for themselves. Each of those things are time consuming and require us to tap into new levels of commitment, so naturally our friendships begin to move in that same direction. Before your 20's, friendships were merely an object of proximity and familiarity. You essentially were friends because the person lived down the street, they were in your class, or you guys had some sort of external thing that played a role in your connection. It reminds me of times when life was so much simpler and the biggest thing on the agenda was getting a ride to the mall with my friends with maybe a $20 bill in my pocket if I was lucky. We'd spend all this time figuring out how to get there just to go buy some Claire's earrings and some Panda Express at the food court. We talked about boys and gossip and there was nothing really baring on the relationship, it was just there, and it was good.

Lessons From My 20's

Juxtaposed to my 20's when everything began to matter about that person sitting across from me. You don't even really realize when it happens but one day you are hanging out with someone and suddenly, the things they say and do are seen and heard so much more clearly and critically. When this begins to happen time and proximity begin to matter less and less and your relationships now become more about compatibility and alignment. Before I knew it, I looked up and a few friendships had just disintegrated over time, ones I would have never imagined I'd lose. If I'm being honest, the relational turbulence that twentysomethings experience is so difficult yet completely unavoidable. And to put it plainly, that hurts, a lot! I empathize greatly with everyone that has already gone through, currently going through, or have yet to experience what it looks like to develop and or maintain friendships during this time of your life. This entire section of the book has been one that I knew I would have to tread lightly in and be sure to hit every key point because of just how taxing friendships can be during this phase. The friendships are not only taxing solely because of loss or betrayals or any other traditional ways a relationship can cause upset in a person's life, though there is often a bit of that too. They are also very difficult because of the sheer unexpected nature of friendships during this time. I have had conversations with so many people that have reflected on friendships in their 20's and the shared sentiment among each of them was just how complex yet invigorating they can be. Overall, there is usually a collective sigh of relief that the phase is over, and they feel much more stability in their relationships now versus in their 20's. The tricky thing about your 20's being a phase where your identity is still having to be ironed out completely is that everything that surrounds you during the transition of becoming your full self is effected in some way by the process. You are introduced to a phase of great uncertainty and your internal self is thrust into so many sudden shifts. This is what makes friendships during this time often mirror a process of mixing oil and water, especially for the friendships you've had since before you entered into your 20's. Keeping friends from the past is a beautiful thing and if you are able to journey through the craziness of your 20's and make it out with them then that is great. If you are not, that is totally fine too. Many times, you feel as though you are losing and gaining friends so rapidly that it can leave you feeling rather empty and alone. This obviously sucks because more than anything in your 20's you want to cling to something steady so that this rollercoaster ride can feel less bumpy. But I can assure you, you are not alone, and things do get easier. Friendships lessen and deepen simultaneously. And that's ok. Lean into it and trust that if you commit to being the best person you can be and continue to grow along the way, the friendships that need to be there will be and those that don't simply won't. If it's one thing I've personally learned about friendships in your 20's it's that you can't prepare for them and you can't teach them, you have to simply experience them. Experiences of friendships during this time are the only sure-fire way to understand, appreciate, and value their depth, complexities, and beauty. So, while writing this I realized I should just share my own experiences that have shaped my views on friendships. In that experience I found that friendships in your 20's can be placed into three categories: Fickle, Fun, Forever.

Raven Martin

Fickle

The research does indeed point to the fact that friendships become more serious and longer lasting but what they don't tell you about is the complex road on the way there. I've found that young people in this phase aren't told that to get to those long-lasting friendships, you're probably going to have to lose a few friends, maybe be betrayed by a really good friend, randomly stop talking to friends you enjoy the most, grow apart from some, and/or outgrow others. No one prepares you for the day that you wake up and realize that this friendship that you hold so deep in your heart and invested your soul into is toxic for you and is not getting you to the next phase in your life, even though you love them. So, whether you know this, experienced it, or haven't heard it yet, let me serve notice, relationships in your 20's start off fickle; but that's a good thing! Let me tell you why! The fickle nature of relationships in your 20's is not a testament on the good or bad nature of people but rather just the essence of what it is to be human in general. None of us are perfect and we are all striving to be our best selves even if some are further along in that journey than others. We are all a summation of our experiences, and we act accordingly. Because our experiences are so vast and wide, our behaviors and matriculation process will sometimes not align with those around us, even those we love dearly. This is a natural part of evolution, and we should all want to evolve. I've never heard a person say, "I hope I am the exact same as I was last year." You don't stop growing just because growing looks like it'll change some dynamics of your life, but rather you grow and go where your best self leads you, even if that means it leads you away from people. It will undoubtedly hurt, and I implore you not to pretend as if it doesn't because that pain is going to provide you with so much wisdom and perspective about future relationships with yourself and others. Don't let it keep you from evolving into who and what you know you need to be. When I lost a friendship that I'd had for more than half my life I felt that pain deep and the way I lost it made it so much worse. But the pain that I had while in the relationship was equal to, if not greater than the loss. I'd known for months that we'd outgrown each other and that it was time for me to go a different route because the friendship was no longer serving me. I stayed however, because I loved them, and I was invested in the time and proximity we'd established rather than what my natural evolution was pushing me towards. It'd gotten to a point where I began to resent the person for them being exactly who they were simply because I'd outgrown them, FIRST MISTAKE! This was the friendship that taught me that I need to take note of all the relationship skills that I develop over time in my friendships both good and bad. The soft skills that friendships teach you will be applicable in every relationship. If you can't thrive in friendship then you won't be able to thrive in other relationships, I assure you. First vital lesson I learned during that time is that you can't get mad at people for doing things you don't like. You can't make people responsible for things that you feel, when you stay complacent about things you know you feel about them or their behaviors. All you're doing is allowing it to sit inside and fester thus allowing self-righteousness to settle in. You're not better than them, you just have a different set of views and behaviors from experiences. When you see that their behaviors do not align with who you are and your value system then you make the decision to leave, respect their

Lessons From My 20's

differences, or call them to the carpet as a friend and be honest about how you feel. Well spoiler alert, I didn't do any of those things and one day we got into a heated argument, and I said everything I'd been feeling for months, all at once. I reached out and apologized and explained everything I'd felt via text. (Sidenote, don't text people when you screw up give them the courtesy of a call. I promise it'll make you a better person and teach you accountability.) Needless to say, I lost the friendship but the lessons I just shared have helped me be such a better friend today and will shape how I approach all my future relationships. Please don't hear what I am sharing and think that I am advocating for you to use people as vehicles to get to your better self. Relationships with people can be seasonal, but people cannot be optional. If you are going to be invested in someone, then invest. If you are not, then don't string people along because it's cruel and inconsiderate of the other person's growth. This experience I've shared was more of one of us growing up together and ultimately growing apart. There is so much I wish that I could change there, just to at least honor our time and love we shared in a better way, but because of the inevitably fickle nature of some twentysomething friendships, the best thing I can do is gain and learn from the mistakes, and most importantly, make sure not to repeat them.

Lessons From My 20's

Fun

I had a friend who I met at work and when I tell you our relationship was the most fun, I'd ever had in a relationship, I mean just that. Even me just saying that speaks to the very nature of our relationship because I love having fun, so I invest a lot of time and energy to make sure I'm always having it; so, to say I had the most fun with her speaks volumes. She was the living embodiment of the meme "Sometimes it's not about years; sometimes it's just a vibe." I won't bore you with all the fun and crazy experiences we had together because they'd easily take up the entire book. What I can say of these experiences, however, is that they are what taught me that those beginning twentysomething friendships, as fickle as many of them may be, can and should invigorate those formative years of your 20's. Formative, because the fickle nature doesn't last always and, in my experience, they are largely in the beginning. You are going to learn from them and develop the longer lasting ones as the more temporal natured ones fall off. Along the way though, enjoy what you can about them and have fun! While in those crappy jobs, ugly and tiny apartments, and rollercoaster ride love triangles, have fun while there. Embrace those around you that are in the same spaces figuring out the same things you are and laugh about it. Fast forward a little bit, this friend eventually ended up betraying me in ways that are too painful to even recall now, but believe it or not, I still recall our days of friendship with so much joy and laughter. While she was in my life, I made the most of our moments and enjoyed all the beautiful things about her. Her betrayal of me reflected a place within her that she hadn't worked on yet, much of which I'd seen while in relationship with her, but I was having a good time, so I turned a blind eye. That blind eye was neither wrong nor right, it just was. Another lesson I picked up along the way in my fun friends' stage. Because much of the topsy turvy nature of friendships is inevitable, it is just best to garner all you can from your relationships even if they are to only last for just a short season. Make that season count. Because I was committed to evolution and intentionality in my own life, we eventually evolved away from one another. I honor her role always though. That friendship taught me that friendships are supposed to be fun, and that I must prioritize people bringing me joy. If you're not

Lessons From My 20's

having fun with your friends, then start analyzing what the foundation of your relationship actually is and why they're in your life. You'll be surprised what you discover. I must say though, the tricky part about the fun friends is that if you are not careful, they can easily consume you and all your time. Because of the uncertain nature of your 20's and the constant transition, it is so easy to create a codependence on good times and comfort. Those friends that you share the most in common and stir up mischief with, are usually the ones that can easily turn into distractions that deter you from your goals. I get it completely, on the days where you know you could be doing ten other things that will get you closer to where you need to be, it feels so much better in the immediate to instead go get tacos with the homie. The fun friends are usually in the same boat as you regarding life and progress, so you guys become an echo chamber for one another, oftentimes supporting mediocrity and procrastination. You have to be really careful to honestly analyze where you are and how much time you spend with these friendships because the nature of them is deceptive and intoxicating if you aren't careful. You will feel as though they are not feeding into your counterproductive behaviors because you guys are virtually in the same place in life, so it gives off the illusion of you guys offering encouragement of progress to one another. In actuality, you are only spending a lot of time with them having a lot of fun and periodically talking about things that you guys want to accomplish—encouraging each other unintentionally to continue in the same old patterns. Fun friends are a requirement and I implore you to find them, but they cannot be the crux of who you spend your time with, especially not during this time in your life. Because this stage is primarily about building, something that is not always so fun, you must be sure to surround yourself with people that can and will push, lead, and guide you as well. They are the fun friend so your natural instinct will always be to resort to fun with them, but ask yourself honestly, is spending all your time with them really going to profit you in the long term? Fun is a necessity in a relationship, but not the only factor.

Lessons From My 20's

Forever

Fast forward to now, while writing this book in my late 20's I can comfortably assert that I think I have found friendships that I am deeply invested in and know for certain are my lifelong or what I like to call, my forever friends. But make no mistake, I am not romanticizing my road to this place. Along the way I have been a poor friend, and I've had poor friends. Because those ebbs and flows happened in my 20's, they naturally felt like death at the time. I wish I would have grasped **Rule #2** a bit sooner because those losses stung, and I went through a phase where I thought I would never develop friendships that aligned with me and what I wanted and more importantly what I needed. Now that I am on the other side of the raucous nature of twentysomethings friendships, I am so glad I didn't choose to forfeit all friendships. You must understand that life is simply way too difficult, while also exhilaratingly fun, to experience it alone. Friendships sometimes just take a few tries and some self-work (we'll get into that later), but they are so well worth it in the end. I can say I most vehemently appreciate and adore my friends now; in ways I did not even know were possible. Culture makes us think that only romantic relationships are supposed to be felt and experienced deeply and intimately. We are told that we cannot engage in relationships that are lovingly close because it is inevitably assumed to be romantic and sexual in nature. Or sometimes we are told altogether that it is best to just forego friendships because no one can be trusted. Media drives the narrative of catty bitches and isolated and reclused men and culture follows suit. All these things are absolutely ridiculous. What my friendships now have taught me is that relationships can be whatever you want them to be as long as they honor and respect who you are, where you are and where you're going. Each of my friends in their own way satisfy my soul and invest in my life and potential in very specific and necessary ways, and I in theirs. I am invested in their futures, and they are equally invested in mine, and I learned how to do that and the importance of that from my fickle and fun phases of friendships. Now the research is coming alive for me. Friendships in your 20's are in fact longer lasting and get more serious, it's just a process getting there.

Lessons From My 20's

Love

"Marriage is seen as more of a capstone than a milestone --- for more recent generations." Meg Jay PhD.

This statement put so much into perspective for me while in my what felt like endless number of attempts at writing this section of the book. I had such a difficult time summarizing how modern-day twentysomethings approach love and marriage though I am actively living through it and deal with twentysomethings of all sorts on a day-to-day basis. Thankfully, the above perfectly encapsulated how modern-day twentysomethings view marriage and helped me so much as I have dug to find what my own thoughts are. The question I was still left with though, was why? What caused the shift in perspectives of marriage? I've got stories for days. I've got good takeaways, revelations, and even what I'd consider universal truths from my experiences, but they are still being tested therefore my experiences weren't substantive enough to answer the question I wanted answered. Why the decline in marriages? This is in fact the age range where marriage has historically happened, and research shows that this is the phase where love and marriage begin to hold precedence in your life. So why? In all my questioning I again sought out the counsel and comradery of my peers and drew from my experiences with twentysomething clients who are largely all in the same boat as I am when it comes to ideas of love and marriage. I found that this place is loosely between, "I know I want something serious eventually and when it happens, I'll just know" and "I want something serious now, but I feel like I am too young to be that concerned about it and I'd hate to miss out on the next thing that may be better." After these endless discussions and research about this teetering we all do between these two realities of romantic expectations, I was still baffled by this seemingly never-ending teetering approach to dating. Still plagued with the questions about why modern twentysomethings approach marriage differently, I decided not to go the traditional route of research because it was leading me down the same paths of understanding. Things like the obvious societal factors and shifts that researcher's far more brilliant than I have fleshed out and are easily visible if you're paying attention, are some

Lessons From My 20's

of the things I wanted to steer clear from. For example, we know as a society we are moving away from religiosity and sacred beliefs that require us to marry and replenish the earth with tons of children, therefore, the shift towards secularism has inevitably decreased the number of marriages. We also know that with the massive rise in women's autonomy and financial independence as years have progressed, the nature of why women marry has drastically shifted, thereby providing them with other options and again inevitably decreasing the number. Other things like different cultures and their perspectives about marriage also play a major role in the decline. Bottom line is, that research has been done and I still felt like there was so much more that was not being accounted for. So, I figured it would be best to just go inward considering I am a twentysomething still unmarried with spotty feelings about love. I figured that since my experience mirrored so many of my peers, I would probably find some answers that also mirrored theirs as well. I began a journey of self-exploration and tried to figure out why I still hadn't decided to settle down and choose "a love" at 27 years old. In my time of reflection, I realized that there were such layered reasons behind why I hadn't chosen a life partner yet and why I continued to teeter between yeses and maybe's. My journey led me to so many more questions. Things like, what do I want in a partner? What has influenced my desires in a partner? How do I feel about my role as a woman in a relationship? What do I believe about gender roles in a marriage? Is there a person who could love me enough to make me feel good about taking such a big leap? To get a better understanding I delved deep into a wide range of viewpoints about marriage, love and relationships. I looked at traditional and contemporary, male and female, feminists and male rights advocates. What I found was both alarming and gratifying. The biggest takeaway was that much of my views of marriage and romantic relationships is rather skewed and damaged. So, I found that what I thought was just confusion about what I wanted in a life partner was actually deep-seated things that made me anxious and outright nervous about relationships. I hadn't personally seen healthy relationship and marriages growing up and so that made me very risk averse to developing one with someone who I didn't believe had the capacity to love me in the way I desired. To this day

Lessons From My 20's

this plagues my mind profusely and makes it so difficult to choose a life partner. Another common theme I found in this exploration was that I'd been clinging to this image of what a prospective candidate would look like. I'd essentially carved out the perfect partner in my mind and really did not want to deviate from that. And finally, and I think this is the most influential of the three, I wanted to feel as though I've accomplished and acquired enough to bring to the table and have something to work with rather than building everything from scratch with a spouse. Each of these things are major factors and at times hinderances in the realm of mate choosing for modern day twentysomethings and even thirtysomethings, though that battle starts to look drastically different as you age. If I had to summarize those three factors in the simplest of terms, I'd say what keeps the modern young adult from embarking on the journey of commitment the same way previous generations have is their desire for better and for more! They saw the marriages that lasted for 50 years and out of the 50, 45 were miserable. They don't want that. They see how their parents were married "for the kids" but secretly and many times openly hated one another. They don't want that. The marriages that could only hold on to one another because they did not have anything else to their names financially to hold on to or thrive with. They don't want that either. The marriages that were invaded by outside intrusion be it cheating or nosy family and friends whose opinions destroyed a relationship they were not even a part of. Nope not that one either. The marriages that were a result of codependence because it's comprised of two people that didn't spend enough time developing as individuals and built an identity on the title of wife husband or parent and nothing else. Not even that one. These are the realities of so many modern-day twentysomethings and I realized that to limit the decline solely to just the shifts in culture would dramatically fall short of the full crux of the issue. Also, it would miss a major opportunity to do some real work around unpacking the layers of trauma that came from the above list and moving towards a place of healing. A healing that could without a doubt lead to healthy relationships and potential families. Believe it or not, research still bears out that most twentysomethings actually desire love, marriage, and family, it's just buried beneath so many adverse experiences that taint their view of whether or not what they desire is attainable. This is in no way a slight to anyone who has been in or who is currently in marriages that are less than ideal, because the truth is no marriage is perfect; not even close. As I've stated in almost every place in this book, and will continue to, nothing worth having comes without work. Marriage I believe is the perfect archetype for that statement. What this is, is an opportunity for young adults to evaluate and re-evaluate themselves, their views, and their goals as it relates to dating, romance, and lifelong partnership. These chapters will provide you with a chance to look at your love choices and examine them through the lens of your inner self and hopefully begin to make better choices that lead you closer to the thriving and perfectly imperfect love life I think we all deserve.

Raven Martin

The Fundamentals

Much like friendships in your 20's, love relationships are largely no different in the sense that they can be very spotty and sporadic while equally being the most wonderful and amazing experiences you'll ever go through. The most complicated thing for most people in all age ranges are matters of the heart. Whether you have lived through your 20's and you're reading this, or you've just started out, dating and romantic love in your 20's will feel like one of the most topsy turvy roller coaster rides you will ever experience. I think roller coaster ride is the best thing to compare love to because no matter how bumpy and terrifying the ride, you still find yourself enjoying, in an inexplicable way, the thrill it provides. Whether it be before you get on, during, or after you've gotten off, you are thrust into an experience incomparable to anything you've experienced before. Love, much like rollercoasters, is truly among the only things that can make you feel exhilarated and happy and equally scared shitless. It can leave you with such an uneasy feeling in the pit of your stomach and you do not know whether to puke or embrace it and hop back on.

Lessons From My 20's

Whether you were married in your 20's or you've never dated anyone in your life, the unprecedented nature of the emotions and desire to partner that most experience during this time leave little to the imagination. This is because of **Rule #2 Chill out, it's the First.** Most are coming out of adolescent years with an experience of what felt like a deep love and infatuation for a person that made them feel as though the world literally and figuratively revolved around that person. Then that frontal lobe starts shifting and expanding and they quickly realize that was their child brain going through the motions of childlike hormonal changes. During this phase of your life, the common sentiment about love you hear is that you are too young to even have a full understanding of what it is. This is so ironic because love in your adolescent and twentysomething years oftentimes feels the most invigorating and sends you through unprecedented waves of emotions. Like anything else in this era of life, you are experiencing rounds of firsts in practically all areas of your life. If there's anything we've learned about firsts in any capacity, it's that they are unfamiliar and therefore cause an influx of heightened emotions.

So as much as we often dismissed the more seasoned generations of people who laughed at our sentiments of love for our partners in our youth, I realize now that they were not wrong. Not entirely anyway. You don't fully know yourself and every time you think you've come into a good understanding of yourself, you are yet again challenged and pushed towards something new. If you are not being challenged or pushed towards new thoughts, ideologies, perspectives, and identities then you need to re-evaluate your surroundings. Love in your 20's is often initially crazy and raucous because as much as your desire for partnership grows more and more keen during this time, your sense of self and self-actualization is growing as quickly, if not quicker. Coming into the realization of who you are is the number one way to have a healthy relationship with all people, but especially romantic ones (meet me in the self-chapter for more on that). Reaching these self-actualizing realizations with a partner, though not a cake walk, is not impossible.

Lessons From My 20's

Take the Limits Off

Before you can even begin dating seriously and exploring ideas of marriage to a singular person, you need to actually date. Love in your 20's, especially around 18-24 is supposed to be rather limitless. Limitless because it should be your mission to meet and expose yourself to all sorts of people and schools of thought regarding love and approaches to relationships. I know people will try and sale you a dream that there is a cookie cutter way to do relationships but there simply isn't. What works for some may not work for others, but the ultimate goal must be to be in a healthy and thriving love relationship that edifies both people. In your early 20's, you should be getting to know yourself and what it is you like and dislike. The only way to do that is by engaging different types of people both platonically and romantically. The thing about your identity not being fully formed during this time is that everything and everyone you experience, both good and bad, contributes to it. I get so frustrated when I see young twentysomethings all bummed out about not having found that Instagram goals kind of love yet. In your early 20's you should have minimal time for that sort of love. You should be so goal oriented and intent on making sure that your future is a solid one you will feel most content with, that finding love will really be a byproduct of the attention you are paying to the betterment of yourself. There is nothing wrong with finding and choosing a love earlier on but there is no need to be frustrated if you haven't because there really is plenty to do and accomplish in the meantime. In saying this, I fully recognize the gender biases and the societal precedents at play when having conversations about dating and self-discovery time in your early 20's. Since the beginning of time, the idea of sewing your wild oats, exploring what's on the market, and taking time to get to know yourself through multiple dating experiences has been reserved for men. Women, as I'm sure we all know, have historically been looked at as used goods undeserving of a good partner if she took this same approach. Though I am not here to litigate how I feel about the gender biases that exist, some warranted and some not so much; what I think is more important is that you get an understanding of what I am advocating for both sexes to do in lieu of these pressing double standards. Prior to settling into something serious, one must get a good grasp on who they are. So, when I implore young people to date multiple people, this is not encouragement to engage in super deep and intimate relationships with a ton of people, and especially not to engage in reckless and dangerous sexual behaviors. I'm proposing the complete opposite position actually. I am advocating for the dating experiences of the formative years of your 20's to be as vast and mentally fulfilling as possible. You can't be your best self for someone else if you have not even taken the time to develop that side of yourself. You don't have to have sex with every person that you go out with or even exclusively date for that matter, you should be gaining dating experience and shaping a romantic identity that will know how to engage a love partner. You better your chances of long-term success in relationships when you take the time to develop a practical experience-based understanding of who you are in a love relationship and what you like and dislike. Think of it this way, up until now, you've only known love and romance through the context of adolescent experiences, what you've seen from others, and media messaging. It's now time to carve your own lane.

Love and partnership are complex and it's going to take a lot more than fluffy feelings to sustain it. It's going to take practice. I learned this lesson the hard way, broke a few hearts, and definitely got mine broken because I hadn't grasped this limitless concept for a while. When I was 16, I met a guy in high school who I'd become sort of obsessed with because of all the trauma that I had experienced in my life. He became a safety net for me in a lot of ways, and at that time I just needed to feel safe. Fast-forward to when it was time for me to graduate and go to college, understandably so I did not want to leave him. Even though the relationship was not an ideal one, and it was highly toxic as we both grew up witnessing highly toxic relationships, I still wanted to stay because he was all I'd known. Because of these trauma bonds, I almost did not go off to school until a wise woman told me, "They're going to be right here when you get back, so don't play yourself." In my mind I was not trying to leave him and all that we'd "established". I found myself infatuated with him and the concept of us being together forever, but that word of advice she gave was so critical and honestly changed the trajectory of my life and perspective. In that moment I

Lessons From My 20's

realized that if I was going to be someone in life and make any real difference in my community, which had always been one of my desires because of all the pain and trauma that I'd gone through as a child, I had to first get away to develop myself. Being consumed too early with a romantic love for another person before even having a clue who I was or what I wanted to do has had lasting negative effects on me that until very recently I was still processing and healing from. What I've often witnessed is that when young couples get connected too early in life, they develop a codependence and interpret their dependence on one another as love. I have no doubt that young couples love one another, because again I was in that very same situation, and I know that I loved the guy I was with. The question however is to what extent are you relying on their absolute presence and commitment to you? Are your goals intertwined with theirs so tightly that you have yet to create any personal plans for yourself? The problem with locking yourself with one person so early on is that you don't give yourself time to know exactly what you want outside of the context of someone else's influence. Think about it like this, all throughout childhood and adolescence someone has been guiding and advising you on how to live your life and what to do and not do. That continued guidance obviously shapes a large part of who we are as people and how we make decisions. Then, if you get into a long-term serious relationship at the first chance you gain a little autonomy in life, someone else is now an active influencing voice in your ear, affecting your decision-making process. Essentially, you rob yourself of the ability to develop full autonomous thoughts and perspective outside of impeding influences. So, when I thankfully went away to school, I saw guys of all sorts. Tall, short, skinny, fat, funny, corny, nerdy, wannabees, intellects, idiots, I mean the full gamut. I was overwhelmed with all the options. Prior to this time, I did not believe for one second that I could love someone the way that I loved my ex, and then I met Him. Tall dark handsome smooth ole Him. I did not know that I could feel so good about a person because prior to meeting Mr. Him, the only experiences I'd had with love were toxic and argumentative. I only saw men in an abusive light, not necessarily even physical but just in terms of talking rough and not being super affectionate. I knew I'd always

Lessons From My 20's

wanted the opposite I just didn't think it was attainable since I hadn't seen it. Oh, until Mr. Him came along. He would go on walks with me around the campus and we would laugh for hours about everything and nothing. He would tease me, and I would tease him, and it was perfect. So here I am, 19 in college away from home, having the time of my life with another man who a year ago I would have never believed would have been possible. Not realizing, it only seemed impossible because no one had ever told me what I want so badly to impress upon you now: TAKE THE LIMITS OFF! Do not confine your love life to the familiar or what you think should and should not be. Whether it be societal standards or family expectations, or even your own pre-conceived ideas of what it should and should not be. I am again not painting too rosy of a picture of this process of understanding. I understand this concept now, but I did not have this full understanding then and I unfortunately created a big mess because of it. I was too afraid to let go of my ex even though I'd felt so much hurt and betrayal from him I was still breaking away from that old way of thinking. In my mind we would be high school sweethearts and be married and live happily ever after. I never dreamed that someone else could come in and upset that at all! Oh, but Mr. Him did and we went through our long share of back and forths with my ex and Mr. Him for a little while. In the end, I chose to leave school and come home to work on my relationship with my ex! I know you probably just called me stupid in your mind. Yes. I was stupid. But the lesson was learned, and it provided me the ability to write these very words and reflect on all this with wisdom. I went the first part of my 20's crying about a man that was always lying and cheating on me trying to hold on to a codependency that I shrouded as love. I limited what should've been my limitless times. As a result of that I went through needless years of stress, trauma, and pain trying to keep a man that did not want to be kept. All of this could have been avoided had I just chilled out, dated around, and had fun. I tell this story not to bash my ex or even praise Mr. Him. Both these men, like all of us, were only a sum of their own experiences. They are both wonderful people now who are doing exceptionally well in their own right, and I have a beautiful friendship with both of them. The point is that releasing myself from my self-inflicted

Lessons From My 20's

expectations and limitations exposed me to something I would have never thought of and catapulted me into learning to expect and receive better from anyone I dated from that point on.

Raven Martin

Rose from the Concrete

For many people, so much of the limitations that we place on our dating lives and expectations from our desired partners is often rooted in warped and toxic perspectives of relationships. Because relationships and love are not easy things to engage in and society really has not done a great job of providing young people with fundamental teachings of what it takes to have effective relationships, so many have opted out of it altogether. The unfortunate thing about that is, it is often not what they want to do but sometimes it is easier to refrain from things that we fear rather than confront and master them. This is so unfortunate because while going through this journey of finding out what influences modern twentysomethings' dating practices, the number one thing that I always found in my later twentysomethings who hadn't seriously partnered yet was a theme of regret. Regretful about their relative lack of urgency in dating decisions and how that has shown up in their lives as they approach or maneuver through their early 30's. What they quickly learn is that as full and exhilarating as your 20's is, they are equally fast, and you must treat them with as much intentionality as possible. After you've spent your late teens to mid-20's years figuring out who and what you want, making the decision to start seriously looking and perhaps circling back to potential suitors is what many later twentysomethings are finding themselves doing or feeling pressured to do. I know that does not sound like the Disney fairy tale love story that told you the process had to be something to the effect of you locking eyes with a person in Starbucks and you both instantly fell in love, but I'd say it's better. You have the opportunity of a lifetime at your fingertips, being able to dismantle all the negative stuff you've seen in relationships and marriages as much as humanly possible and carving out your own relationship and how you want your future to look. That shouldn't be left up to chance and fairy tale ideas. The only ideas that count are the ones you feel are best suited to you. When I hear young people say things like "we're not our parents' and grandparents' generations, we want happiness and marriage," I am heartened that they have enough fortitude to carve out a new lane and choose contentment over complacency, but I worry that this does not tell the whole story. I fear that in trying to secure relational happiness for themselves they risk their opportunities at lifelong companionship looking for a perfect love. Essentially, they may be sacrificing the good for perfection. Furthermore, though I agree societal expectations of love and marriage have evolved since our parents' and grandparents' generations, we don't necessarily have to do away with the positive aspects of those unions that came together to eventually get us here. The bottom line is there are pros of traditional marriage and family and pretending to be oblivious to them does not make them any less real. If it is your desire to be partnered and produce children from a union you develop with a partner, then it is crucial you explore both the good and bad aspects of marriages from previous generations. I'm reminded of the adage, don't throw out the baby with the bath water. If you are a child of divorce, a toxic marriage, unwed parents, domestic abuse, emotionally neglecting parents, or any other aversive love experiences, then you have double the responsibility placed upon you to master those traumas (I'll tell you how later) and create the love life you want and have always desired. The thing that is going to be most tricky for young adults with these sorts of experiences is

Lessons From My 20's

that they are going to have to set their sights and intentions on what they actually want and not just what they don't want. As a child of a loveless marriage, I know all too well the feeling of running away from what I saw, seeking momentary or temporary thrills to compensate for the love I so desperately wanted to experience. It is easy to become so hung up on all the negatives about love and relationships that you either end up doing exactly what you deplored in the first place, or you forego love altogether under the guise of some cheap excuse. "I'm just looking for the right person that can handle me." "I'm going to meet someone, that's just not my focus right now." "I'm just working on myself right now because these (insert gender pronoun) aren't good enough out here." How many times have we said or heard a variation of one or more of these responses from people who we know have relational trauma and who are also getting to those later years in their 20's. All these statements are perfectly fine responses, remember I am a proponent of taking genuine time to make sure you have a working and healthy understanding of yourself. So, these assertions can be easily accepted, but when under the context of trauma with love and relationships there is almost always something more to the hesitation. That something more must be confronted because you only do yourself a disservice when you continue to pretend as though relationships are inconsequential to you. Just so we're clear, this is not my elevator pitch for marriage, though I am admittedly a strong advocate of it. What it is, however, is an opportunity for self-reflection; an opportunity for one to access themselves and find out whether their anti-marriage sentiments are rooted in hurt and fear of failure and pain. I can assure you fear of striking out will not prevent your regret in playing the game. I've been in session with so many clients, particularly men, who have expressed their disdain for marriage or confusion about its relevance altogether based solely on what they've seen in their own lives or the images that have been placed in front of them in high stakes marriages that have ended in sour divorces. They usually make the case of how the man more times than not loses everything in the divorce and the woman gets to walk away richer and happier. To them I say yes this is often the case and unfortunately there is no foolproof way to prevent that. I am not naïve enough to even attempt to present a rosy picture of marriage or anything for that matter, the reality is it is one of the most consequential decisions you will ever make in your life. But I'm afraid that limiting your view of marriage to the possibility of its miserable failure, is just too narrow a view. The reality of marriage also consists of having someone there during your most joyful and painful times. No one wants to experience tragedy alone and not contending with that reality for expedient fear of it is a major risk. I advocate for deep self-reflection time like this because it can really aid in preventing the sour outcomes as much as possible. It will help you become self-aware enough to first require that same level of self-awareness from your partner, ensuring you all have better chances on being better more integral people in the world and to each other. Second, it will help to create boundaries, guidelines, and promises to one another that you both adhere to. Again, nothing is 100%, but taking that extra time in your early 20's to get to know yourself and develop a person who is actually decent and good and moral is so important to help prevent those sorts of issues. The bottom line is, get to know yourself and be fully honest about the things about you that are not so ideal or that have been tainted by things that you've seen. Only then can you truly say you've given it your all and come to any conclusive decisions about something as monumental as choosing to partner for a lifetime with someone. Whether or not you are choosing to opt out of marriage or even lifelong partnership altogether, one thing I urge all young people in this age group to realize are the feelings of loneliness and a longing for lasting and substantive conversations and bonds that start to settle in as you age. This is not a consequence of anything other than simple evolutionary biology. We were designed to be in community with one another and as we age life gets more and more serious and isolated for so many people. Right around 28 and 29 people are starting to settle down, have children, and go into overdrive in their careers and life journeys; all things that require one to step away from the fast-paced nature of a younger twentysomething. When this happens those silos that you'd already felt begin to develop, maybe after you completed high school and definitely college years, are magnified. I've had conversations with so many young people that get to this

Lessons From My 20's

point and feel as though they are on an island all alone and it starts to scare them in a way they've not experienced fear before. They begin to realize that all the great and wonderful things about their youth have come and gone and like it or not they're bodies and minds are shifting them to a new place. This place is not a negative one and it's not one to be angry with, it's just new, but more on that later. What I hate to see happen, is a young person get to this place in their life and realize that they have not spent any real substantive time thinking about who they'd like to partner with because they felt as though it was not important or worse, out of running away from painful memories and experiences from the past. Those later twentysomethings and early thirtysomethings that I've encountered all have expressed a trend in their sentiments, they have a bit of regret not starting the process of choosing a life partner sooner. Your brain is evolving and will evolve into something that wants something more meaningful. That may not look the exact same for everyone, but everyone certainly experiences a variance of this. Those nights with random people partying or meet ups and hook ups get old and the desire for someone to know you, see you, and care for you grows what feels like overnight. Unfortunately, though, the ability to develop that sort of bond with someone does not come overnight, leaving many who start to feel this way with feelings of deep loneliness. With those feelings of deep loneliness often come a string of irresponsible partnering decisions followed by equally irresponsible sexual ones. This then becomes a cyclical process spiraling further and further into isolation. One of the renowned fathers of psychology, Erik Erikson, calls this stage intimacy vs isolation. This theory asserts that those who don't develop loving and intimate relationships during this time are statistically more likely to experience this loneliness and even depression. This is personified many different ways in people, the first one that I see so much that is also very deceiving is in the cases where people are overly promiscuous. This means they risk their personal health and well-being in their sexual experiences. Excessive risky sexual practices are usually just an outward expression of a deep internal longing. On the surface it would look as if this were done from a longing for partnership though I'm sure that is part of it, I'd say, even more

Lessons From My 20's

so it's a deeper ache. A longing for connection that satisfies those internal wounds they feel. Wounds from those painful experiences, wounds from feelings of inadequacies and insecurities, and so much more. This can be very deceptive because how can there be a longing for something, and a person be experiencing isolation, and yet they are always engaged with another person? What happens is that the sex is usually used as the instant gratification needed to either mask the feelings or ignore them altogether. As much as popular culture is moving more and more away from healthy sexual ethics, in my experience, the lion's share of modern-day twentysomethings still desire monogamy and struggle immensely with the thought of long-term sexual promiscuity. Another way I see this isolation personified in twentysomethings is many of their tendencies to choose isolation and commit to becoming somewhat of a hermit rather than creating and participating in life. This happens romantically as well as in their social lives or lack thereof. This is often shown in twentysomethings, particularly male, who spend most of their free time on video games or the females that consistently stay home instead of making time for social recreation.

In the present, these long streaks of loneliness and isolation can feel manageable and more comfortable than the energy it takes to mingle and develop intimate love and platonic relationships, but in time most find the isolation crippling and eventually destructive to their overall wellbeing. Our hearts were made to give and receive love and intimacy. If you're going to choose to forego these natural human proclivities, make sure you are prepared for all that comes with that decision. Your mid twentysomething self may be comfortable with it, but what about your fortysomething self? You can give them a voice and a say so now.

Lessons From My 20's

Self

There is no way of knowing yourself in your 20's, not fully anyway, but that's no excuse to forsake yourself and the journey of establishing who you are. Your 20's are a decade filled with wonder and wander and it's a never-ending journey of self-discovery. As soon as you feel like you know yourself well, you get introduced to a new part of yourself that fascinates you even greater than the last. The smartest thing to do is to build upon the information garnered in the last round of discovery and begin to create a whole person out of the fragmented and scattered pieces. In this process what you are doing is creating a self, a self you feel most comfortable presenting to the world. The problem many young people have is that they are either trying so hard to be conclusively one thing or they use self-discovery as a means of circumventing the responsibility of creating themselves. Instead of giving themselves the grace and the privilege to evolve and working hard to find themselves, they simply leave it up to chance, many times unintentionally. This is because evolution can be scary, many times thrusting us into the unknown. People find themselves running from it in hopes to hold dear to the portion of themselves they know best. Finding later that it often happens at the expense of their greater self and their highest potential. I say this with full understanding of the difficulty of this process. The self is a really tricky thing to discover and in your 20's it is a completely life altering experience that, if not carefully done, can lead many on a counterproductive and even destructive path. Who I am today is almost completely different from who I was in my early 20's. Who I am politically, religiously, spiritually, emotionally, mentally, physically even, has been drastically transformed and I am more and more amazed and afraid by the transformation every day. Amazed because I love who I am becoming because I know that I've put in work to develop and evolve myself. Also, I am stunned at the stark contrast. You couldn't have paid me to believe that I would adopt some of the views I hold today. Nevertheless, here we are. I am afraid at times because if I'm honest, it is easier to stick to what you know. Evolving who you are takes hard work, exploration, commitment to adventure to an extent, and most importantly a removal from what is comfortable. I've done that

Lessons From My 20's

and continue to do that, even at the price of not being liked and accepted by certain peers that I've adored for years. With that, I had to realize, and I tell my clients and everyone else who'll listen, your 20's is a phase of life that asks a lot of you, more than most phases. You are essentially trying to create the life that will sustain you for the duration of your life but with the framework of an adolescent because that is the only other way you have lived up to now. It's literally like being forced to build a real house that you, your spouse, and children can live in with the same tools and pieces from the playhouse you played in, in your parents' backyard. Because of this, it is so important to engage in new experiences, lessons, and relationships in your 20's in order to create this new person and life that can withstand the coming decades. Rigidity is not going to build up that capacity in you, and neither is indecision. It's going to take a good amount of open mindedness along with discipline to get you to build the stable foundation these coming decades will require. In every other decade of your life, you'll have already had the prior knowledge and experience of "adulting" thus making even the unfamiliar and/or painful facets of the next ones not completely earth shattering (it doesn't have to be). However, during this one, you're going to have to build from the shards of other people's experiences, shoot in the dark a bit, and walk forward until you start to develop your own rhythm. It's scary but not impossible.

Lessons From My 20's

Who and what do you want to be really?

Culture hasn't given us the tools necessary to dive into the conscious self. We're taught to shut off feelings, grind and hustle at the expense of our sleep and personal relationships, obtain obscene amounts of wealth at all costs, and survive with the illusion of happiness and this will somehow suffice. This leaves us with people that have checked off all those boxes and if not literally, they've mastered the art of pretending to have done so. Yet depression rates are rapidly increasing and the feeling of arrival for most is still a distant ideal only brought about in peoples' illusionary lives. Breaking free from the illusion and stepping into full actualization of self will not be an easy task because of how we're socially engineered to do the exact opposite, but there are absolutely steps to take to begin the process. I think the first is simply acknowledging all the places where you put on a front to either impress someone or uphold a standard placed upon you by something or someone else. We are no good to ourselves by not being exactly who we are. This is difficult many times, because again, we are hardwired to live with our real selves filtered so much that we become unrecognizable to ourselves. We adjust to the deception that the altered version of ourselves is a more comfortable setting despite the continued feelings of inadequacy and our very evident feelings of the inability to level up we experience. Because of these feelings we unconsciously try and make ourselves more palatable for other people all the while stripping away our real selves and exacerbating the feelings of not belonging. Once we decide that who we are despite the filters and unrealistic expectations is worth exploration, the sooner we can embark on the real journey into growing up and finding ourselves. We can get to that place of self-actualization that so many desire but many never reach. It's often never reached because a lot of this place of actualization that we desire is really born out of all our innate needs and inherent desire to be seen. If we lived in a world where people felt seen rather than like failures, then we'd be a much more emotionally healthy society and twentysomethings would feel far more equipped to handle the transition they're thrust into. This desire to be seen has left so many hanging in the balance of lost identity and victims of group think, and even worse, group behavior. Group think and group behavior is a more sophisticated version of elementary school peer pressure. In an effort not to be set apart and run the risk of isolation and invisibility or worse exile, so many twentysomethings simply adopt what the masses say, and think and do. I have seen this personified so much in our current political and social climate. Differing viewpoints that do not align with the more mainstream and popular narrative are immediately discarded and people are made to feel like social pariahs. The group says one thing and it takes a great deal of strength and courage to differ, so many young people just choose the road most travelled. This happens intentionally but many times it happens unintentionally as well.

Before I made transitions in my thought process about who I was as a person, I found myself inundated with the way that the people around me thought and what's worse, I didn't even recognize it. I'd adopted all that encompassed my worldview from my family and friends and had never really questioned it seriously. I would find myself arguing for points and perspectives that I hadn't even fleshed out within myself, but yet I felt so strongly about. I realize now that I was doing so because I'd had these thoughts and sentiments for so long and they had sentimental value to me. When developing your identity, sentimental values and views that you hold near to your heart are important, but they are not the only things that should influence you. As you age, you'll find more and more that there are so many people around you with a ton of thoughts and viewpoints and it would be in your best interest to critically and seriously explore them. I had to learn that just because something means something special to me does not give it accuracy or legitimacy in the world. If I was going to build my identity on things, I needed to have a healthy balance between truth, facts, reality, and the traditions and patterns I was born and bred into. The goal, no matter who you want to develop into, should always be to produce a whole, healthy, and well-rounded person. That type of person is not developed by holding on to thoughts and ways of being without critical analysis and deep self-reflection. Again, I know that this is not an easy process, and just like with every other thing in this book, I don't offer it as a task callously. I fully recognize that the time and mental wherewithal it takes to critically

Lessons From My 20's

analyze something about yourself and your worldview in order to develop your identity is a first world privilege that resources and environment make easier to complete. That said, it is still possible for everyone who is living and breathing and can be done by simply looking at your life from its start to now and thinking through who you desire to be. Being willing to challenge yourself to get a better, more evolved version of yourself is always worth it.

Raven Martin

Commit to Kindness and Integrity

In my journey to self-actualization, one of my most consequential and life-altering takeaways has been my relationship to kindness and all that it produces. Not only does it produce warm and fulfilling feelings within me, but what it does to the world around me and everyone I interact with is noteworthy. While finding myself and figuring out who I wanted to be I had a phase where I neglected my character and integrity for expedience and convenience. During that time, I thought I was a good person because I didn't cheat or lie or kill and steal. I figured I covered the basics of what it takes to be considered a "good person," so I was ok. It wasn't until I was confronted with situations that called my character into question in unprecedented ways. A friend of mine lost her father and during her time of grief I did not reach out to her in the way that a true friend would. I sent condolences and offered myself up to her in a simple and subtle way because I was afraid of being one of the many people that I knew she was being bombarded with. Essentially my pride kept me from going above and beyond to make sure that I did my part in assuring she felt loved and supported from me, regardless of how many people were outreaching her. I don't usually like to feel like another number in the bunch and I let my prideful feelings supersede my duty as a friend. You may be thinking how this calls my integrity into question, and that question is the whole point. It isn't an easily pointed out integrity flaw, but it was still evidence of a more deep rooted one, which was pride and selfishness. That friend called me out on my neglect of her in those days and from that day on I've tried so hard to be a better friend and overall person. This is why I felt integrity and kindness needed an entire section, commitment to it is not just about confronting the basics of good and bad that we've been taught. Commitment to integrity is about challenging your norms and committing to being the best person you can be internally. Recalibrating who you are even if you feel as though you are good where you're at. The world is filled with people just trying to get by and in many cases, many will do whatever it takes to do so. That does not necessarily make the world filled with bad people but rather just that, people. Once we enter adulthood, we have a responsibility to be intentional about moving beyond our own personal needs and more towards a holistic people centric view. You don't do this at the expense of yourself, but rather you navigate the complexity that is caring for yourself and your fellow humans. You must commit to seeing them as a reflection of yourself and treating them accordingly. That is true integrity. That is true kindness. Another instance where my integrity was called into question in a life altering way was during a time where I was dating a guy while still having very strong feelings for another man. Though that has its obvious flaws, I am not saying that this is always a deal breaker, but in my case, I hadn't closed the chapter completely yet. I was waiting on the guy who I still had feelings for to come and essentially sweep me off my feet once he had his act together. The guy who I was dating in the interim was a magnificent man with wonderful qualities and I felt deeply for him, but just not in the way that I did for the other guy. I excused my poor decision making away because in my mind I had every intention of leaving the previous guy alone and fully committing to this new guy, but it just did not happen that way. So, in that moment what I did was make excuses for why we could not be,

Lessons From My 20's

and I basically convinced him and myself that he was not adequate for me when all along the main reason was because I was in love with someone else. To this day I regret it deeply because it was completely unfair. I hurt a wonderful person and dishonored myself and my so-called integrity. During this time might I add, I was still professing to be a "good person". My point is, we all believe ourselves to be good people until we are challenged with the nuanced scenarios that require us to choose between bad, semi-evil, and outright monstrous. Some would argue that it is situational, and I'd agree because integrity is simply not black and white. I was hurting and confused and had never felt the true loving embrace and warmth of a man, so I embraced someone who gave this to me not realizing at the time that I was not ready to reciprocate. Does that make it ok? Of course not. But I have come to recognize that context matters when judging integrity and nothing is ever black and white. Commitment to these principles is not about getting it right all the time, but rather being intentional about making it a fundamental part of who you are. When circumstances arise that challenge you morally, you more readily revert to the choice that is most integral and good because your value system you have been developing makes it next to impossible to choose the alternative.

Lessons From My 20's

Trauma

The vast majority of my 20's was spent navigating the ramifications and residue of traumas that I was subjected to for much of my adolescent years. In every relationship and interaction, I'd find myself having to review hurts and pains that I didn't even know existed. At every milestone, both positive and negative I found myself unable to fully embrace or contend with them because they would trigger old emotions that I had not dealt with. Every conversation, every dollar attained, every realization developed, came with it a set of pains and confusion. If I had to create a rank sheet of the most important things to do in your 20's, unpacking and addressing your pains and trauma would easily hold the number one spot. So many times, what I've seen with more seasoned adults that were unable to take advantage of all life has to offer is that their traumas are what crippled them and left them in limbo regarding who and what they are and want to be. So though working through much of the pain I experienced as a child and beyond was difficult, doing it during the phase where I was already in development was opportune because it gave me a chance to not only feel it but to apply those feelings to the practical lessons I was constantly being thrust into daily. I am by no means saying that I am completely healed or moved on from the things that have caused me hurt, but rather I've learned how to healthily navigate the feelings and most importantly how to use them. When I say trauma, please don't think it must be some stereotypical catastrophic event that happened to you per se. Many times, peoples' minds immediately go to something like abuse, neglect or some variance of the two. Though those are two examples of trauma, they are not limited to that. A trauma is defined as an emotional reaction to a negative event. They are not uniformed in any way other than that they cause adverse reactions to the people they affect and ultimately affect our lives so much more than most people realize. In my experience, people who by all accounts would be considered rather emotionally intelligent are still unaware of the ways in which their traumas have impacted their lives. Many times, people aren't even able to identify why they are incapable of certain things or respond to situations in an abnormally particular way and that's largely because of unexplored feelings related to a trauma or

Lessons From My 20's

overall adverse experiences. So, I learned in my 20's that you not only must identify them but dissect and explore them thoroughly so that you can have a working and active understanding of their impact, not just for the sake of knowing, but to make sure that they don't hinder you in unintended places. My first serious boyfriend in my life was a direct reflection of who my father was. He was stoic, emotionally damaged, well-intentioned but incapable of properly emoting feelings and/or showing love, affection, and commitment in a meaningful way. At the time of choosing him I had no idea that he was a spot-on reflection of my dad. I had heard all the people say that women date their fathers, but I had not put any real stock in the thought, especially not while picking my boyfriend. Nevertheless, there I found myself dating an essential replica of my dad, with a few exceptions. From that relationship developed so much unhealthy codependence and tolerance of full-on nonsense that I should have left long before I did, but because he identified with some unexplored traumas and triggers that were brought upon from my father, I stayed. Even once I made this identification I still stayed long after that because the connection and codependence had already developed. I felt almost as if I needed this man to survive, not physically, but emotionally. That relationship lasted for so many years because I had gone so much of my late teens and early 20's just moving about trying so hard to outrun my traumas I'd experienced from my father, rather than sitting with them and working through them. From 17 to about 24 I was moving so quickly to create a life that was completely opposite of all the pain that I'd experienced, I hadn't even taken a moment to review it long enough to even know the extent of what I was running from. My unwillingness to explore it left me with more pain than I started with, only now this pain was more self-inflicted and dangerous. It was dangerous because I was attempting to mask it with the same sort of things people and behaviors that caused it. The same kind of man as my dad, the same kind of emotionally avoidant behaviors that I witnessed from him and my mom, and the same sort of relentless seeking and acquisition of things to make me feel whole. Think about that for a second, I spent the entire first half of my 20's in what I recognize now as a fake world. An emotional illusion if you will. I was shut off from my actual feelings and trying to create an alternate reality to make myself feel better. I'd discussed the realities of my problematic childhood and pains of the strained relationship with my father with positive figures in my life, but I hadn't contended with how it made me feel. I would review what I call "the story" repeatedly, sit in it briefly, and become overwhelmed and hurry to try and move on from it or make myself busy with a way to compensate for the experience. For example, I'd be asked about an experience or a specific pain surrounding our strained relationship, I'd recall a story and get slightly emotional, tamper the emotion down immediately and dismiss it with a more productive thought. It was usually something about an accomplishment I was working towards or trying to convince them and really myself of how resilient and unphased by it I was. It was and still largely is so uncomfortable to sit and think about how much those experiences affected me and pained me deeply. Looking back, I honestly give myself grace for the way I tried to compensate in those moments now, because I fully recognize the weight of difficulty that goes along with exploring pain, especially in a phase of life where you are tasked with building a life and an identity out of the shards of what you acquired in your adolescence. All I wanted was just to be happy and to start to try and create a better life for myself. So, the idea of returning to those places and days that caused me so much pain seemed sort of counterproductive. Nevertheless, I tried a few times in a few different ways but exploring them felt like too much emotional labor that would lead me nowhere. In my mind exploring my pains looked like exposing myself to the anger and sadness that I was already familiar with and once I was finished exploring them, I'd be left with more anger and sadness and nothing productive. This is a large reason why so many people either do not contend with their past pains or get stuck in them. The problem with that approach though is that you will find yourself running from something you do not understand and if you do not understand it, then you really do not know how to master it. If you cannot master it, you're doomed to perpetuate it even though you had no intention of doing so. I was trying so hard to make a relationship work with a young man that was clearly not interested enough to make it work with me. Had I taken the time to explore my traumas and pains

Lessons From My 20's

related to my relationship with my dad, I would have found the similarities in their behaviors and picked up on the warnings as well as the causes for both their toxic behaviors. For example, upon my personal exploration process I learned of so many traumas that led to my father's inability to love and emote the way I needed. Those led him to be more emotionally and physically abusive than I'm sure he would've liked to be himself. As it relates to my then boyfriend, the same sorts of experiences happened to him, therefore making it next to impossible for him to love me the way I desired and deserved. From both those realizations I learned so much about how men handle trauma and react to adverse experiences as opposed to how women do. Had I come to those realizations earlier, I could have realized much sooner that I was not going to be able to make this man love me because he does not know how to love and honor himself yet. Granted, I was in my early 20's so I'd argue that it takes time to come to these sorts of more critical understandings, still the lesson remains true. I perpetuated the very traumas I was trying so hard to get away from. It's the age-old tale that we see in every drama film, kid leaves abusive home to get away from the abuse they grow so tired of and ends up with abusive partner. This is a more overt example, but the principle applies in whatever area a person has experienced emotional adversity. If left unexplored, you leave yourself and your whole life vulnerable to its effects. And at that point, no one is responsible for what comes of it but you.

Lessons From My 20's

How to explore your trauma

I share a very concise and condensed version of my story and dealings with trauma to drive home the point, but in doing so I don't want to present the process of dealing with them in a serious way as an easy thing to do. I fully recognize that it takes time and emotional strength that is hard to tap into, especially surrounding matters of the heart and issues that have pained us. But difficulty is never a good enough reason to not do something, particularly something as consequential as healing from hurts to create a better life for yourself. That said, I believe there are steps to mastering traumas. Note, I said mastering and not overcoming. Before we identify how to explore them, you must come to terms with the fact that you will never be fully over it. Therefore, you can't overcome it. I know the world would, specifically us work 'til you drop westerners, have us all to believe that if we work hard enough or acquire enough then we can whisk our pains off into oblivion. Hate to be the one to break it to you, but that is just not true. The literal definition of overcoming something is to *succeed in dealing with a problem or difficulty; defeat an opponent.* Your traumas start off as opponents that you feel you must defeat and success relative to their existence seems like you are prevailing over them or despite them, but in my experience those feelings of conquering and defeating them are only temporary. Trying to overcome them leaves you with the expectation that you must be over it eventually and that is just not going to happen. Furthermore, what happens on the days after you thought you had gotten "over it" that you experience deep sadness or engage in reckless behavior as a result of the feelings or thoughts you experience from them? You are left feeling worse about yourself and the trauma than you were prior, leaving you to explore feelings of disappointment in yourself now. I believe the better way to approach trauma is to acknowledge that it happened, and it caused you great pain, that pain then became an archive of your life that helped to form your identity into what it is. So essentially, it will never be over, but you can master it. There are three ways master can be defined and all of them are immensely better definitions with which to navigate your relationship with your traumas.

Lessons From My 20's

It is historically defined as: *one who has people working for them, especially servants.*

As an adjective: *having or showing great skill or proficiency*

As a verb: *acquire complete knowledge of or skill*

Each of these definitions in relationship to your traumas are reflective of something that can be healthily worked through, managed, and repurposed for great utility in our lives. Gaining knowledge of your trauma will help you to use it to your advantage. It aids in the process of not being a victim to it but rather someone who can take the very thing that brought you discomfort and turn it into a catalyst for something better. One moment where this became so clear for me was back when I was 20 years old. I had an abortion with no support from my ex who had gotten me pregnant. I was devastated and embarrassed to say the least, that I had let myself get to such a place that I thought I'd never end up and especially without the man to support me in the first place. Many words were exchanged, and things happened during that time between he and I that hurt me deeply and with that painful experience and many others that reverberated from it, I developed a platform that gives stories like mine life and space to be explored. What I am saying is really the age-old tale, turning your trauma into triumph; do not let what you've been through define you; turn your trial into a testimony. We know all the euphemisms surrounding traumas and moving through them but in my experience that is normally where our capacity around them ceases. The reality is the average person is largely emotionally immature and the world we have all cultivated really has not given us the tools to deal with our positive and negative emotions. As a therapist I have seen so many of my clients come in struggling to even identify words to associate with feelings. I cannot recount the many times I have asked something as simple as how does/did that make you feel and clients respond with a story about what I asked about or a message they got from it, or even a thought they had surrounding it, but never about how it felt. Attributing feelings to the adverse experiences you have is the first step to mastering it. When you give an experience a feeling you create an association in your mind

Lessons From My 20's

of what that situation and others like it brought to you and you are better equipped to work through and master it. Ultimately what I am saying is, learn to know your trauma in a new way beyond the negative experience. It is incumbent on you especially during your 20's, to wrestle with those traumas in a meaningful way because like it or not they are most times the larger contributing factors of our lives. For the longest time I could not figure out why I would go so hard in life. I recognized that hustle and grind are necessary in life if you want to acquire and achieve things, and as a black woman we're socialized to work until everyone, and everything is taken care of. However, my longing to acquire and achieve cut a bit deeper than I could grasp for a while. That is until I reached a point of awareness and realized what was driving it was my need to level up because I never felt as though I leveled up enough to the point of recognition of my family, particularly my father. I wanted so badly to prove to him that I was not going to be the statistic that ended up in dire situations needing help with things and relying on other people. These were the people that he shunned all my life and no matter what I'd do, he would treat me as if I was one of those same people he despised. So, for the longest time I don't think my mind really grasped that and I was left always reaching for affirmation and acknowledgment from him that I was not failing. That never came. So, I left his home and came out into the world with something to prove to people that had no stock in what I had going on or the things that had caused me pain. This is something I see so often with young people; they think they are chasing after something and showing out and the reality is they're running from the past and showing the world how hurt and unstable they are. Are you chasing or running? This is such a pivotal point of realization for twentysomethings because I know how easy it is to get engulfed in the expectations of the world. So many lose out on what they actually desire because they are running away from something someone said or something someone said they should or shouldn't have. My whole life and everything that was driving my need to succeed was something negative. Trying to prove something to someone else left me mostly fighting the air. I came to find that nothing was ever going to satisfy me because my driving force was what I was running from. I didn't even know

Lessons From My 20's

what I wanted; I just subconsciously knew what I didn't want to be. Furthermore, because what was driving me was negative, what I did and how I treated myself along the way to my perceived "success" had no boundaries and standards. I wanted to be successful to prove him wrong instead of actually measuring what success looked like for me and from there creating strategy to acquire it.

Raven Martin

Addicted to the story:

At one point, I'd become largely obsessed with the story of what had happened to me and what hadn't happened for me. This led me down a path that I have seen replicated by so many of all generations, but it is one that can be squashed if addressed and defeated early, becoming addicted to the story. "The story" is whatever adverse happening or lack of happening for you that resulted in you becoming or adopting portions and or versions of yourself and your life that you dislike. One of the greatest things that I learned quick is that your traumas are your own and that the world is not entitled to coddle your aches and pains. This may sound cruel, but it is actually to your benefit that it is this way because it helps you to become resilient and to learn the art of self-soothing. Furthermore, when you face them head on you have the opportunity to either do something about them or wallow in self-pity and create excuses for why you are incapable of doing something. Identifying traumas should be used as a tool of explanation of certain characteristics of oneself, not excuses. Once something is explained to you then you can properly handle it and move about in the most educated ways. When we use our traumas as excuses for bad behaviors, indecision, laziness, and apprehension like many young people do, we are doomed to a cycle of self-loathing that will leave us unfulfilled and discontent with ourselves. I have seen this story too many times to count. Older adults living with so much discontentment about their lives because they allowed their "story" to create the confines around what they could and could not accomplish. It is never too late to accomplish things or to go after anything that your heart desires, but life does create windows of opportunity and over time windows do become more and more smudged, so when opportunity knocks do not allow shortcomings that were of no fault of your own to keep you from progressing. It is important we remember that everyone has a story. Everyone has had some sort of adverse experience in their lives that has shaped and affected them in a substantial. Whether or not one is more traumatic than the next is irrelevant. The point is that to be human is to experience turbulence at some point and for many, turbulence at many points. We are all entitled to some degree of suffering and the true character of a person is defined solely by how they handle and master that suffering and the trauma that will ensue from it.

Lessons From My 20's

Reality

Throughout many of my conversations and interactions with twentysomethings one consistent theme became very clear, there is a looming fear and anxiety about the concept of getting older and being saddled with more responsibilities. Among the many anxieties and fears that come along with this age range, the one I've gathered that most encapsulates the share of them is the uncertainty of what it really means to be an adult. What I've found is that much of that anxiety is dismissed by different factions of age groups. Younger people dismiss it because they don't quite understand it yet and they only see twentysomethings lives as a free and autonomous one to envy. Older people typically dismiss it because in their minds they have already made it through that time and so often they look at our anxious antics as mellow drama that needs to just be worked through, or a bit of envy as well; envious of the youth they have, and all their presumed time left in the world. I think this is where we as a culture have errored with regard to how we help young adults navigate adulthood. The thought that you are aging and are now coming into a world where you are

100% responsible for your life and livelihood is an enormously large pill to swallow, even if you're more accustomed to independence than others. I'm sure that much of the continued spiral into isolation and nihilism that many twentysomethings are moving towards can be alleviated if more attention and intention was given on the part of generations that have passed through this time. Whether or not they moved through their 20's with great ease or they struggled the whole way through, hearing firsthand non-condescending advice and experience of a person who's made it through their 20's provides so much more security and assurance than most people realize. In an ideal world, every twentysomething would have a mentor that outreaches them and gives them advice on what critical steps to take financially, romantically, personally, etc. The reality though, is that if you never get that sort of guidance, you are still solely responsible for yourself and the outcome of your life. If no one ever steps in and provides you with the blueprint or a well-versed manuscript on what it means to be an adult, you are still responsible for making sure you create something out of nothing in your life.

Lessons From My 20's

Yes, growing up and becoming an adult is the most scary and difficult thing you will probably ever be forced to do. Even scarier; there is nothing you can do about it. The only alternative to aging and all that comes with it is death. That seems dark and morbid of me to say, but I fear that many twentysomethings have yet to contend with this truth. It may feel dark, but this is a large contributor to that rising number of depressive disorder that we are continuing to see from coming generations of young adults. Those feelings of inadequacy to do what is required of adults leave many instead just floating in the realm of indecision. Indecision about so many consequential and life altering things, but as with **Rule #4 Indecision is still a decision**. That fear and discomfort with the thought of aging and responsibility must be contended with. They are only as scary as your reluctance to confront them and your life seriously. We were physically designed to handle the responsibilities that come with becoming an adult. As we age, our brains continue to develop and right around the time where responsibilities begin to thicken and what is expected of us heightens, our brains are simultaneously developing and becoming more equipped to handle complex thought and develop long term strategy. All I am saying is that you can do this. What too many end up doing is becoming overwhelmed with the thought of responsibilities rather than taking it in bite size pieces and digesting the expectations one at a time. This is not an all or nothing sum game. I fear that is what many twentysomethings get wrong. After being inundated with images online of people seemingly having it all, when they are incapable of attaining that same thing, they fold under the pressure and the feelings of failure. Yes, it is going to be hard to build a life. Yes, there are going to be really frustrating days, and you are going to feel like you don't know what you're doing on most days, but you have to just keep moving. I wanted this section to be nothing but a sobering reality check. Good lives are made, and you must develop thick skin, critical thinking skills, a spiritual connection, and a healthy body to live and thrive through this life.

Lessons From My 20's

Cry and Move

The world looks at you through the lens of what you can produce and judges you by your level of utility in it. That is not a fun thought. That is an overwhelming thought. But once it is accepted, the sooner you can get to developing who you want and need to be. After committing to hard work, committing to being a good person in love and relationships, and starting the process of mastering your traumas, you now have a responsibility to just adult. What that means can feel tricky but it's really not. The societal markers of what enters someone into adulthood that we have set in place are for the most part in line with our age. Earning a living, paying multiple bills, moving on your own and taking care of yourself are some of the more standard things that depict entry into adulthood. I know there is a faction of twentysomethings that struggle with these fundamentals of entry but there must be concrete decided markers for there to be real structure because they are vital to the survival of a civilization. In my quest to find out why so many struggled with these fundamental entry way rules I reviewed my own time as a younger twentysomething until now and my feelings about being thrust into so many responsibilities. I was one who has always been relatively on my own. While staying with my parents, aside from food and shelter, I purchased and navigated everything on my own. I was pretty adept at responsibility and the art of making it happen for myself. However, even with what I'd consider a great amount of experience doing things and earning money to sustain myself independently, I remember days where I'd become so overwhelmed with deep sadness and frustration about having to continually figure things out. There was one day, where I'd gotten into a car accident. I was 20 years old, and this was the first car I'd ever purchased, and my first car ever. It was a 2003 white Chevy Malibu. I'd bought this car by saving up a few checks from my job at Ross Dress for Less. For context, the car was I think $700, and it took me three checks to purchase the car and the plates, so you can imagine it had great meaning to me. As I was driving home from work one day after having the car for only a few months, someone hit me and drove off. I tried as hard as I could to chase after them, but the shattered pieces of my car could not compete, so I ended up pulling over on the lot of a local KFC and sat there for quite a while. I cried. Oh, did I cry. I hadn't felt that confronted by my own feelings in a very long time. In that moment I felt all the weight of what it was to be a budding young adult, solely responsible for making it happen in her life, with no one to provide any substantive safety net. On that day I was introduced to, in a new and very real way, the realities of becoming an adult and I felt ill-equipped. I keenly remember being overcome with feelings of bitterness and anger at the thought of not having anyone to come "rescue me". Not just rescue me from the scene of the accident, but from the realities of responsibilities. I knew that once I left that place, I'd be responsible for dealing with those feelings of loss and anger at everything I'd worked too hard for and purchasing another one. In that moment I cried and left the lot with my already raggedy, now totaled white chevy malibu left behind. On this day and a few others like it, I felt crippled by the thoughts of me being solely responsible for the outcomes of my life and that only increasing as the years progress. I know this is a central theme of fear for young people and for many it is highly debilitating. Many opt out altogether not because they like the feelings of stagnation and immobility but because what it takes to become an adult can feel really scary and many literally feel incapable of it. That thought of no one caring about you not having it altogether or being willing or even able in many cases, to lend a hand because you are at the age where you are expected to be moving in the direction of having it together can be terrifying. It feels as though the world is increasingly looking at you with the expectation of you needing to figure it out and anything short of that feels like a disappointment to you and everyone to whom you are connected. You want to know how I made it past that crippling moment? I allowed myself to grieve the childhood that was no longer there. I cried and reflected on the luxury of relative carelessness I was once able to live my life with. I didn't allow my fear of the unknown that came with adulthood to cripple me into stagnation. Yes, I was afraid that I would continue to take losses even in the face of my continued efforts to win. Yes, I was angry that I had two living parents but yet both were incapable of coming to my financial or emotional rescue when life was at its most thick moments. However, I knew that failure was not an option. I knew that I had a vision for my life and in order to bring that vision to fruition continuing to move forward was the only option. When twentysomethings begin to feel those somewhat inevitable feelings of crippling fear and anxiousness about the future it is key to first recognize **Rule #2 Chill out it's the First** so that's why these losses during this time can feel more debilitating than they are. After contending with that, they must realize that life will only be as good as their resilience. If you allow your mind to be overtaken with the setbacks you will face during this time, then you will never do what it takes to master the discipline and wherewithal you're going to need throughout your life. Your 20's is the time to create and cultivate those foundational tools that help you fight adversity, self-motivate, and discipline yourself to move when all you have the energy to do is sulk. In all my feelings of overwhelm I honestly did not know how everything was going to turn out, but I always held a fundamental understanding that no one was going to "adult" for me, and apathy was simply just not an option. The only other option was to cry and move. If I had to summarize my answer to how to become an effective adult, my answer would simply be cry

Raven Martin

and move because things do not fall into place, they are put into place.

Lessons From My 20's

Spiritual Identity

Mainstream beliefs and narratives will have you believe young people, particularly twentysomethings, are leaving spiritual and religious affiliations in droves. Granted, the stats do bare out the fact that this is the least amount of religious practicing young adults in history, but I believe that a major layer of context is missing from that narrative. As someone who spends her time with twentysomethings and who is currently one, much like all stats without the proper context or essential deep dives, you miss what's most important about the fact. I am always curious about the why behind everything, specifically the things that make assertions about a whole group of people. The stats about how young adults engage religious and spiritual matters would lead one to believe that they are a rather Godless and solely secular group of people. Even in mainstream discussions among older generations, young adults are often presented as lacking in morality and character. Many would even go as far as to say that they do not have a value system thus making them susceptible to do anything. Historically speaking this is a normal response for older people to cast wild, some accurate some not, aspersions on the generations following them. These sorts of thoughts are often asserted in response to the more liberal behaviors that younger generations naturally gravitate towards. History has shown us that people get more conservative as they age so when your grandma yells at you for not being married by now, or for your clothes being too tight, or some other things they may fuss about, it is really as to be expected so try not to take too much offense. As generations pass, we get more and more desensitized to things that were once considered taboo and we evolve out of whatever the defining marker of conservatism was from the previous era. Simply put, it is easy and on brand for an older person to constitute the ways and behaviors of the next generation as unruly or worse, ungodly. As a Christian who was born and raised in church, I could not tell you all the many times I've been confronted by an older person who condemned me for something that I'd said or done that they deemed as not "Christ-like" or representative of my faith. The reality was that much of my presumably poor behaviors were not a reflection of my distance away from God or all things good and holy, but rather a direct product of me growing up and creating a lane for myself in this world. They were largely what I think are the missing pieces of the argument around young adults leaving their faiths, which is their longing and desire for something more. So much of what we've been presented with as God, God-like, or spiritual has just been perceptions and traditions of what some people believe are right and wrong. Though there is value in traditions both oral and written, what is more important is that we allow ourselves to grow and evolve into the awareness of the need for a connection with our spiritual identity and with God. I am in no way advocating for anarchy and recklessness in your behavior as you grow because the more missteps and mistakes that can be avoided, the better. But the reality is, missteps and mistakes are inevitably going to be made so it's best to use them as catalysts to draw you closer to the infinite parts of your being that are divine and connected to a force far beyond any sources of abilities, power, and potential we have access to. Because there will be days that you feel most defeated, no matter the amount of encouragement you provide yourself, you must have access to something larger than yourself when all else seems to be failing. Your spiritual identity is the crux of what makes every other message in this book work and come to life. That tenacity I discuss, the resilience and journeys of self-discovery can only be done with your soul postured in the place of humility and openness. Open to acknowledge that you are finite and that you need something greater than yourself, you need God. Only God can take your gifts and abilities and magnify them to the highest degree. You will begin to capitalize on your dreams and visions for your life in ways you never thought were possible as a result of a connection with the divine. What I know for certain is that many twentysomethings are simply searching for more. They are actively seeking deeper and more meaningful connection. That connection I believe is something existential and so much larger than the traditional religious context previous generations presented. Many times, this age group is often presented as wanderers moving about aimlessly with no moral foundation. I think its deeper than that. I think the wander is a direct reflection of the search. Young adults are developing identity thus they are seeking what best suits their needs, in this case their internal

Lessons From My 20's

longing. That longing is often filled with more temporary things leaving them with feelings of emptiness that often lead to a deeper search, one that is often left unfulfilled. With the rise of globalization and access to unprecedented waves of information immediately at our fingertips, the options for spiritual guidance became endless and quite inevitably with that, the appetites increased. Much like anytime any of your satiations are overly stimulated and presented with multiple options, we of course opt out altogether from an inability to settle on something. This is in fact my fear of what has happened with twentysomethings. A wave of spiritual and moral relativism settled in, and it was ushered by adverse experiences with God and religious organizations. As a result, there are generations of young people who haven't the slightest clue about who they are beyond the external things they can touch, feel and see. With that I must say though, I get it. For years we've watched and heard stories of outright horror with regard to the way people were treated in the name of God and religion. So, a deviation from all that is even remotely reflective of some of the nightmares we've witnessed is understandable, to say the least. So many have been forced to abandon what they've always known and identified with in pursuit of something better and more fitting to the person that they are becoming. I know that zealots have tried to paint that as an easy thing to do because of Godlessness, but I know firsthand how difficult it is to abandon things and associations we care deeply for when they don't meet our expectations. Those expectations are there because it's innate for us to expect nourishment and goodness from sources that were made to provide it. To some degree it is a loss that has to be grieved. After that grieving period though, it is paramount that young people take that pain and the lessons learned from those experiences with religious affiliations that many were brought up in and begin to create anew. In my conversations with twentysomethings, I find a consistent theme of relinquishing their religious identities in search of a more connected and personal experience with something beyond our physical limitations, the existential desire is the lure. I have been in so many conversations with many friends and peers after nights of drinking, or watching something very thought provoking and the conversation always

Lessons From My 20's

resorts to a variation of this question, which is often borderline an assertion, there's got to be something more, right? What they've seen historically has scarred them in lasting ways and the thought of joining in on something as rigid and oftentimes stoic as any particular religious affiliation is a major turn off. I know how easy it is to hear something like that and cast it aside as someone who is young, careless, and perhaps who wants to live life on their terms with no guidelines and boundaries, but I can assure you it is deeper than that. It's more like a desire for some supernatural semblance of assurance and hope. Hope and assurance in the fact that life and all things both good and bad within the confines of it are not actually left up to chance but rather there is something, someone, or some people group that are working beyond our earthly capacities. These concepts are scary for some and unbelievable for others, but the fact is we all have an existential longing if we are alive and breathing. A spiritual itch that must be scratched. I can personally identify with this spiritual reckoning a great deal and I know firsthand that longing to connect to something greater than myself. I found myself caught in between that place that so many young people find themselves, the crossroads of what you've always known religiously and the need to jump out of those confines and limitations. I was raised in a traditionally Pentecostal/Apostolic black charismatic church and everything that you'd imagine would come with all those adjectives, double that. With that, I was raised under very stringent rules regarding lifestyle, behaviors, and practices. Everything was seen through the lens of not sinning and doing everything in your power to not sin. Essentially the message of the gospel was largely replaced with legalism and duty. Because of this I was relegated to the mindset that my faith was rooted in things that I did and said and anytime that I deviated from that model, I would feel a sense of guilt that would loom over me so heavily. As I got older and became a budding twentysomething, I started to see the error in this approach, so I slowly started to inch away from it and started to form my own thought around what is right for me spiritually, though I was still so steeped in legalism and bigotry in so many ways. When I entered college, one of my good friends was rather liberal in her views and during our time together she taught me a

Lessons From My 20's

great deal about agnosticism, history of Christian imperialism, and her personal experiences with sexism and isolation in the church. Some of the stories we would swap with one another about the different abhorrent things we'd witnessed or personally experienced in church astonish me to this day. Afterwards I found myself completely turned away from the church and all its ideals. I felt as though I did not need it to be a good person and it did not define who I was one way or the other, so I stepped away from my faith. For a while I would profess to be largely unaffiliated and that I was just trying to be a good person. I'd made the assertion that I did not need to identify with Christianity or any God for that matter but rather I could just be my best self and conduct my life in the matter that I saw was best. I know that the more climactic and expected progression to this story plot would be that I eventually ran into a brick wall and had to go and crawl back to Jesus begging to be back in good graces because I'd seen the error in my ways. Unfortunately, that is not how the story went at all, but I'd say the way it progressed is even more profound. One night I was away at school, 400 miles away from my hometown and not in touch with anyone from my home church at all, barely in touch with anyone from my home. On a Monday evening after I'd been engaged with my more liberal friend for a week, now deeply enthralled in this new philosophical thought of secularism, I decided that I was going to walk away from my faith completely. I'd been thinking seriously about the idea for a while, and would even acknowledge it to myself personally, but never really had the courage to acknowledge a full rejection of the faith to anyone publicly. I was frankly afraid, not of any particular person, but just of the power in the assertion and the relinquishing of something I'd always looked at as vital to mine and everyone's being. Monday night comes and I get a text on my phone from a woman who goes to my church that read, "Hey good evening, I know its late but give me a call when you get a chance." I think nothing of it more than she just wants to check on me maybe she is thinking about me since it has been such a long time since she's spoken to me. I plan to call the next day but in true college freshman fashion I was preoccupied with all the activities and my life and forget to call. The next night comes, she texts again and says she would love to talk to me when I have a second and to

Lessons From My 20's

make sure that I call her the next day. I text back and promise not to forget. In my mind I'm thinking ok why is it that serious, I still didn't think much into it though because maybe she just was reminded that I hadn't called and wants to send a gift or something. Keep in mind all the while I'd made the decision in my mind that same Monday, she sent the first text to me. I was certain that I was walking away from my faith for sure and to be honest I felt really good and empowered by it. At the time I felt as though believing in anything was silly and for non intellects. The next day, I forget to call again and lo and behold the next night I get a call from the woman at my church at around 12 or 1 am and this time I am at a concert. It is loud and she could have easily just heard the concert in the background and chosen to wait one more day, but she insisted that she could not. This time she was in somewhat of a panic and says that she had not been able to sleep since Monday night. She said she had been trying to refrain from calling because she did not want to seem weird or out of place as she did not have a close relationship with me to call me and assert anything about my life. But this particular night she says she felt as though God wouldn't even let her lay down without calling me first and delivering this one message. The message was simple, "Do not walk away from your faith." In that moment all I could do was drop my phone and break down and cry, like violently cry. In the middle of a concert with people all around me jumping up and down in this extremely loud and dark space, I came to know something so much larger than a religious affiliation. I'd come face-to- face with my soul and my spirit. I was making the decision to choose secularism wholly and profess that spiritual concepts are dated and unnecessary, but the way that my body experienced that moment of reckoning from that phone call was something I could not describe. There is no way she could have known that I was on the brink of making this decision and for all the intellect and insight that I'd been developing, nothing was more refreshing to my inner self than this moment. It was and will always be one of the most profound and life changing moments in my entire life, forever changing my worldview.

Lessons From My 20's

There is More to You

Our beings are so complicatedly beautiful. Yes, we are humans wrapped in flesh and will absolutely be relegated to the ground when this life is over, but what I think so many dismiss is that the human experience is only part of the journey. There is more to our existence than just living and dying, and I worry that isolating that spiritual part of ourselves leaves our lives, our potential, and our capacities vulnerable to the limitations of our temporary nature. There are portions and phases of our psychological selves that require wisdom and understanding beyond what we can muster up naturally. There are levels of hope and joy that can only be achieved by way of something outside of your physical capabilities. Days will inevitably come where no matter how many lessons of resilience you've mastered, or love and hugs you've received it will simply not be enough to walk through the darkness and sadness that you'll feel. In that same vein, there will be crossroads and milestones that you will reach that will require insight from beyond you. Your spirit was built to grow, love, expand, experience and persevere and when any of those things are not working at their full capacity you feel it deeply and your life usually reflects just that. This is a sure sign that there is something so much larger at play relative to our existence, and we all have a responsibility to access it to truly be our best selves. The consequences of not contending with your existential self are, in my experience, far too great. I don't say that suggesting anything bad will inevitably happen to anyone who chooses the path of secularism or to not believe in the idea of a soul and spiritual identity; I just mean that I've seen so many people with such great potential slip through the cracks because they were incapable of tapping into the parts of them that would have taken their good to great and great to exceptional. A wonderful example of this is when young twentysomething men particularly seem as though they are incapable of moving beyond a place of apathy and complacency in their lives. We all know the guys, perhaps you are one, who are tied to things, thoughts, patterns and behaviors that they had in their teenage years and feel literally incapable of moving beyond. To many in their immediate circle, like their family and maybe a few friends, they may be looked at as lazy and not serious about life which then leads them into even deeper fits of complacency and feelings of incompetency. They often do not want to be that way and definitely don't want to be looked at as losers who can't make anything of themselves, but the thought of trying to move forward and take on the responsibilities of dominance, leadership, and provision that society largely expects from men is petrifying. So, what many do is hide away and resort to the lowest and most familiar denominator, complacency. Complacent with what little money they are bringing in, complacent with the sexual and romantic interactions they've gotten thus far even if they aren't ideal, and complacent with the way they are perceived despite how negative they may feel about it. They relegate themselves to isolation so that they do not have to be confronted with this unsatisfactory reality. The root of all this behavior is often fear. This sort of fear is justified because being a man in our society is hard and often left without a great deal of blueprints for various reasons. That level of crippling fear can only be remedied by coming to the understanding and recognition of a capability larger than oneself. A capability that can only be accessed through a relationship with God. The things that it takes to successfully be a man and thrive in this world as an adult are characteristics that can't be gathered from a book or academically, it's going to take a yielding to something greater than oneself. I know that in the hierarchy of life men have always been at the top as it relates to delegation of responsibilities. Regardless of one's thoughts and views on that, that is what so many men have internalized and so many fold under that pressure. What so many of them see is themselves at the top with no recourse or assistance but what they miss is that they are to answer to God and resort to their spiritual self and connections for strength and accountability. Those feelings of isolation and depression that so many fall into can be largely mitigated if this was pushed just as much as the list of responsibilities that they are told they must adhere to, to be deemed a man of value. God is the way you acquire and strengthen those characteristics of strength, courage, leadership, wisdom and bravery to go out into the world and thrive in your respective space. It's scary because it's not to be done alone.

Lessons From My 20's

Countless studies show that to believe in something larger than oneself has so many positive effects on our bodies and our health. There have been studies done that show terminally ill patients who were connected to a spiritual belief beyond themselves, and their physical status had better outcomes in terms of overall wellness and joy throughout the process of their sickness. The studies did not show that the prayers or the belief guaranteed anything for them but what they did in fact show is that belief in something provides hope, and hope in and of itself is a supernatural state of being, one that transcends where you are presently. To have hope is to acknowledge that there is possibility for more, even in the face of nothing reflecting that. Some may say that this is naive, but I'd argue that it's the awakening of our greatest selves. The study shows people getting better and feeling better not because God loves one person more than others but because hope and optimism is a medicine to our bodies provided only by our souls. That realm of yourself can only be activated through acknowledgement and active work at identifying with your spiritual being. When days come where, God forbid, sickness, death, or tragedy befall you or ones you love, it is this very hope that will do the work of propelling you forward when all you want to do is stop. I know some may read this and question why I'd classify this hope as something spiritual. They may feel as though hope is just something that we possess naturally as humans and there is no need to add a spiritual component to it to make it any truer. To that I offer you this, think of just how unthinkable and difficult it is when you experience a devastating loss or betrayal or any life shattering pains and traumas that are inevitably apart of the human experience. There are experiences that are so life altering that they have the power to (and for many have) drive people to change their lives completely or take their lives altogether. Those sorts of unprecedented and painful responses to those experiences are like out-of-body experiences and they feel like nothing any human should experience. The fact that we are able to experience tragedy on such inhumane levels to me is indicative of the fact that there are levels of joy, hope, optimism and resilience that are equally beyond our own capacity. There are places where only a connection with a God larger than us and any other forms of support can bring us from. Just as there are losses and tragedies that will shake your core, there are also wins and milestones that must be contended and grounded with something larger than oneself. Things like coming into great wealth and success or being fortunate to have children and a family are examples of life changes that will require insight and skills that cannot be gained within your own realm of capacity. Because we are human, we are susceptible to human tendencies which include a great deal of vulnerability in the area of falling victim to greed, excess and pride. God and the concept of having a source of power to be held accountable to helps to put and keep things into perspective for us in a way that is needed as human beings. We have a natural tendency to want to be our own boss, live by our own rules, and move how we want and feel is the best. This is only dangerous when left to our own devices, because we are so finite and driven by physical desires. You can set your sights on whatever path you feel is best, but I'd strongly suggest developing a relationship with God so that those decisions aren't left to your innately limited and flawed perspectives and insights. I know in the age of modernity and secularism; moral relativism is widely accepted and the thought that humans should have the autonomy to live and do as they please on an individual level and needing something to be held accountable to is not the most popular of notions. My idea of accountability is not in the traditional sense that I and many like me grew up in. I am not advocating for some stringent message of legalism that forces people into archaic standards of living for the sake of religiosity and rules. I am making the argument for connecting yourself to a safety net, one that helps to keep you and your most vulnerable state in alignment with and under full subjection of your best self. As humans, being responsible to exude character and strong ethics all the time is simply too difficult, not because we are inherently bad but because we are inherently flawed. We are human. We need something larger than ourselves to hold us accountable because nothing temporary can bring other temporary things into subjection. It's really basic laws of existence. You are made up of so much more, so you must seek more!

Lessons From My 20's

Bad Religious Experiences

You must contend with who you are on a spiritual level beyond superficial and external things because that is how you fully sustain your external body. Having a spiritual connection is far beyond normal weekly church, mosque, synagogue, or temple attendance. It is your acknowledgement that you are a soul much larger than the confines of this earth and it is now your duty to create the space that is reflective of what we naturally crave. I've seen a common theme among twentysomethings that have the desire to be a part of spiritual communities and feel the existential desire, but they've been so deeply turned off, hurt and disappointed in former leaders, people who professed a faith they once held dear, or just in news headlines. Many felt a deep sense of betrayal because they'd once held their religious and or spiritual beliefs at high regard either personally or just as a matter of social reverence and were privy to egregious things that turned them completely off. Maybe you felt like spiritual leaders are supposed to love unconditionally and not judge, yet you were a victim of harsh criticism by one in particular. That was not ok! Maybe you felt betrayed and lied to by someone who professed to be a spiritual person. That's not ok. But you must know that the longing to fulfill those existential desires you have will not go away simply because you walk away from anything resembling a faith system. It is up to you to reconcile those feelings within yourself to fill the longing! Looking for perfection in religious people or affiliations is not the answer to the upset you are feeling or experiencing. The world is made up of imperfect people seeking hope wherever they can grasp it and that includes people who affiliate themselves with religions. You must now contribute to or create a trend of individuals striving for love and self-progression. No matter the experience you had with religious people or places that may have scarred your image of God, they are all made up of hurt and broken people, and guess what, so is every other arena. Let's just be transparent because, 10 times out of 10, that person or persons you're angry with have similar if not identically mirrored struggles as you. You can be of assistance to them or to the next girl, guy or group on your journey of evolution. For some reason your faith walk towards your spiritual identity did not happen ideally for you and that's not, nor will it ever be, fair. However, life is not about fairness, it's about getting better. Make those spaces what they are naturally supposed to be because that's how you fulfill that deep existential longing in your soul and spirit. Not revenge, rebirth! Show up, infiltrate, look inward and determine how the outward should look. Abandoning God and spirituality and replacing it with a bunch of temporary empty behaviors won't make the longing disappear. The world is about persistent evolving and that includes the people who are also seeking to fill the same longing you have, even when they get it wrong. Again, I say emphatically, what happened to you should not have happened to you and you can contribute to the certainty of it not happening to anyone else. But rest assured, if you don't take those negative experiences and use them to turn your deep longings for God and something more into actions that make other people's spiritual journeys less difficult, someone else will and in your contempt and apathy on the sidelines all you can do is hope that somebody somewhere will come along and change or "be better" for "them." You are them. They are you. Better is in you.

I think young adults have such an amazing opportunity in front of us, one that allows us to really reset the standard for what God and spirituality look like! We have been bred in a generation of information, knowledge and understanding that the generations before us just did not have access to at no fault of their own. Let's use that and rewrite the negative narratives. God is inclusive, God is loving, God is smart and welcomes intellect. We are Justice Seekers and the hands and feet of God. We can continue to complain about what we dislike about the religious people and rebel, or we can create the atmosphere that we all want, one that is permeated and overflowing in love! That longing for deeper fulfillment is rooted in something so much deeper than I think so many realize. There is a larger issue at play when it comes to people's tire of religious and spiritual practice. Go with me as I try and piece together what I think is a phenomenon we must address if we are to see any real progress and create spaces conducive for people to move forward and get that existential healing and reckoning, we all so desperately crave. What is most innately human, among other things, is our desire to be loved and cared for, understood and valued, respected and cherished. Most important of these, I think, is to be loved. In society, there are certain pillars that we all subscribe to instinctively because that's simply the way we've been engineered. For example, when people have children, we anticipate parents loving and nurturing them, likewise with teachers and school children, customer service reps and consumers, pastor/church leaders and congregants. It's one of those things that, although no one has ever seen these sorts of relationships done without flaw, we still expect those traits in abundance from people in those positions. When any of them fail to perform in a way that is to our satisfaction or that is hurtful and disappointing to our expectations, we immediately throw up our hands in disgust and repudiation to that person and in this instance, entire institutions. We give no room for failure or error. It's because in each of those relationships mentioned above, you're providing a segment of yourself that is of great value, and oftentimes not just readily available and on display or given away.

In those relationships we naturally resort to the offense, as we feel as though we no longer need to be so defensive and have our guards up. We are in anticipation of being poured into and cultivated. We are ready to experience greater and pushed into better. One thing for sure, hurt and/or betrayal are not on the list of expectations from these interactions. The key now is figuring out how to grow beyond these moments of human error because truly that is all it is. The sooner we allow ourselves to empathize with even those that have brought us pain, the sooner self-actualization begins. I in no way intend to be dismissive of experiences, quite the contrary, because the first step to effective empathy is empathizing with self-first. Not dismissing experiences. Acknowledging how hurt you've been by said institution or person, then allowing yourself to be angry and hurt with intent of linking it to purpose is key. Anger and hurt without plan or purpose turns swiftly to bitterness and dead weight that leaves you going out on a weeknight getting sloppy drunk to "escape" that perpetual feeling of emptiness and irrelevance you have been unable to shake. You get home and sit with your friends still questioning the meaning of life and are still plagued with the "why we all are the way we are" and "whether or not this is the life you

Lessons From My 20's

feel you should be living questions." Or you get home alone and STILL cry; you still feel that same emptiness only now it's quiet and yet blaringly loud because the silence is sobering and the mood enhancer (sex, liquor, drug, etc.) only magnifies that hollow place. Your indulgence of this (insert drug of choice) is a personification of this painful emptiness. That pain and hurt inflicted on you was never meant to lie dormant, it was meant to be repurposed. So that questioning and emptiness will remain until you reckon with and not run from it. And just a side note, reckoning with it is not constant complaining about it every time you see the opportunity to drag the religion or spirituality. That's just pain that's well past the repurposing expiration date and now rotted and settled into staunch bitterness. Growing up religious, this is a reality I know all too well. Feeling as if I've lost my ability to go back because of a compilation of things that I allowed to happen to me, and some things that happened to me completely out of my control. I knew some of the things that I know now but at the time my knowledge was coupled with a betrayal that my 19/20-year-old heart and my brain just could not sustain. On top of the presentation of the age-old question we all have at some point "Is this even real? Is God even real" Beyond those questioning moments though, my point is simple, it's easy to abandon things when they don't meet our expectations. Those expectations are there because it's innate for us to expect nourishment from sources that were made to provide it. So yes, grieve it and empathize with yourself because you were wronged, and you should not have been. Period! Now, it is your duty to create the space that is reflective of what we naturally crave, because it is necessary. Become what you needed and need.

Lessons From My 20's

Fountain of Youth

The day that I came to grips with the fact that I was not going to be young forever I may or may not have had a breakdown. I honestly don't remember the exact time because to this day I am still finding new ways to process such a staggering reality. I know I was not alone when I asked, whose idea was it for humans to have to grow up? Whoever forced us to age and become adults should really lose their jobs because they clearly aren't that great at it. During your 20's, if you are fortunate enough to have all your bodily functions working at full capacity, the process of aging and getting older is one that I know many twentysomethings feel like they do not have to think about. You are still largely at the prime of your adult life, your metabolism is still pretty good, and all your organs and internal functions are at their peak. So, unless tragedy or unforeseen circumstances take place, many are skating through the phase carelessly in terms of their physical health as well as how they approach those around them. I get it, if you have lived a relatively traditional

Raven Martin

twentysomething years and your life went in normal sequential order, then this is more than likely the first time in life where you have a bit of autonomy in your life and the first instinct is to flee the nest and live your best life however you see fit. Eat whatever you want, call family only whenever you feel necessary, some call only when there is a need, some choose not to engage at all. Many feel as though this is their chance to dismiss any thoughts of the past and the way that it affected them and chart a new path away from all they've known. So many envision this high life with high expectations and aspirations, many times with no real plan or goals to reach such levels of expectation but the youth is the driving force. The youth, which comes with health, invigoration, potential, energy and excitement sets them in this place of euphoria and they function their lives out of this frame of being. Quite honestly, I think that is beautiful because those are some of the most beautiful benefits of youth, the access to dream and live in the excitement and promise of potential, or what I like to call the fountain of youth. This fountain of youth is a relatively miraculous place because it is filled with what is almost like magical water that allows you to eat poorly and not be affected by it immediately. It creates a framework where people pity you in your youthful naivety and give you second and third sometimes fourth chances to get it right. This fountain affords you the opportunity to be in process of "getting it together" whatever your "it" is, without too much judgement and heat from the outside world; not any that would hurt more than your feelings for the most part. It affords you mistakes and slip ups and confusion. This fountain I'm telling you is magic, and it essentially lays the world at twentysomethings' feet and provides them limitless opportunities. The trick is though, it dries up. One day eating that third slice of pizza will actually affect your health in long term and serious ways. One day, that open bottle of liquor in your cup holder while you are driving is going to get you caught up and you will perhaps lose out on a major opportunity. There will come a day where people are less impressed by your gift of gab and won't give you the benefit of the doubt when you make a mistake. What you presently produce, is going to be more important than what your potential is eventually. Afterwhile the world will look at you as another full-fledged member of society and either you are an asset or a liability. Like it or not, both have real consequences. Assets get respect, liabilities don't. I know this is a place of real anxiety for so many, but it needn't be. Once you come to terms with the fact that this fountain does in fact dry up, you can milk it for all its resources and that way once that time period passes, you'll have already gotten what you need from it to move to the new places awaiting you. There are best practices and strategies to interacting with this fountain. Just like with every other thing we've discussed thus far, living, and moving with intention is key to developing and maintain a thriving life throughout adulthood.

Lessons From My 20's

Health and Wellness

When I went to college, I like so many who go, gained what is commonly known as the "Freshman 15," only by the time I'd gotten through my freshman year it was more like the "Freshman 22." I'd gained a great deal of weight because I was eating much more poorly because the cafeteria food was available to me, and my schedule was much more autonomous than it was in high school. I was super active in sports and other activities in high school, and I also did not have nearly as much access to the unlimited food supply that you are introduced to when you go off to school. I would eat anything I wanted, and I had no real discipline in my eating patterns. Not only were my eating patterns poor but I also spent the first part of my 20's completely ignoring my persistent health condition. I was diagnosed with hypothyroidism when I was a little girl forcing me to be on a medication every day to replace the thyroid hormone I no longer have. Your thyroid is a gland in your body that produces all the hormones you need to function. Well, if you no longer have one and you are not on any supplemental medications for long periods of time there are serious consequences to your daily functioning. Coupling my neglect of medication along with my poor eating habits, as you could imagine, was a very irresponsible thing to do. However, at the time it did not really feel as though that was the case. I still felt well and aside from not really liking the weight that I was gaining I still felt moderately ok, so I thought I was fine, and I continued my habits. Time progressed, and by the time I was 23 I was about 210 lbs., for context, that was about 50 lbs. over what my normal weight was, and I was starting to have real life health consequences from going years without taking my medication as well as gaining a substantial amount of weight. My vocal cords began to develop nodules when I'd sing because my throat was perpetually dry causing me to strain and go hoarse very easily. That year I'd lost my voice for the entire summer. Bear in mind I was an active singer at my church, now incapable of singing and barely talking. That's not even the half of it, I started to have Multiple Sclerosis type symptoms. My whole right side would go completely numb, my hands would tingle, and I could barely make a fist on most days. One day I was at work, and I started to struggle to walk down the steps and nearly fainted heading back to my desk. I eventually scheduled an appointment with both the ear nose and throat doctor for my vocal cords and the neurologist for my MS like symptoms, both doctors ran extensive tests. They gave me advice and made preliminary diagnoses, they then both asked me in what is now an unshocking tone, "Oh you have hypothyroidism?" I responded, "Yea, why?" Both doctors in both appointments explained to me just how vital it is to be on my meds and how without consistency with them all my organs literally cannot work at full capacity, causing many of the breakdowns and problems I was experiencing. The vocal doctor then went on to tell me that it looked as though I had also been experiencing acid reflux due to my poor diet which was causing the vocal cords to decay from the strong acidic fluids. My neurologist explained to me that once I got on my thyroid medication, all my MS like symptoms would more than likely go away. He also encouraged me to start to eat a more balanced diet so that I could begin to replenish some of those missing hormones and functions in my body in the absence of my thyroid. I share this story not to be pejorative to anyone struggling with their health or even with body image issues. I recognize how real and prevalent those issues are and I don't for a second take them lightly. I share it to simply shine a real and needed light on a more serious issue and principle that caused me and so many others to dismiss the real risks and dangers of not investing in your health early, that's just simply ignorance. So many young adults are ignorant to the seriousness of health and wellness, and they often take for granted a healthy body until it is no longer available to them. I've seen so many people in their 30's and 40's suffering from strokes, heart attacks, diabetes, and so many other chronic illnesses. Many of them forced to scramble to try and create healthy and balanced eating habits and exercise regimens because they neglected to develop those patterns early on and it eventually caught up with them. While in your 20's you do have the luxury of sort of floating by neglecting your health, eating what you'd like, and not experiencing the consequences right away. However, what so many fail to realize is that your body and all its functions are beginning the process of aging even though this is just the early stages and the beginning. You do not feel it right away but rest assured that the process is happening whether you pay it any mind or not. If you don't start to develop healthy lifestyle habits in your 20's it becomes exponentially harder to develop them later. No, it is not about being small and aesthetically pleasing to critics and for Instagram likes, but it's about your body being in the best shape that you can possibly be in so that you can do all you can in your power and means to live a healthy and thriving life. When I went to see the neurologist about my body going numb, I really thought that I had MS and that I was on a slow decline in my health, as MS is a degenerative disease. Though that sort of disease is not caused by poor diet and exercise habits, that moment in the doctor's office was still very sobering for me. I realized that, up until that time, my health wasn't serious to me until it had to be. I was mindlessly gambling with the one thing on earth that I have the most control over, all because I arrogantly, naively and ignorantly felt as though I was going to be healthy forever. Looking back on that time I can honestly say I never envisioned a day where I would not be in good health. So as my body started to betray me in that time, I became afraid, and something awoke in me. I got back on my medication regularly and I started the process of eating healthy and working out regularly. Over the course of about a year, I lost 52 lbs. and I got my thyroid levels to a much better place. My voice has been restored and all of those numbing and feelings of fatigue went away completely. I now workout on average 4 times a week and I eat a balanced diet. I eat vegetables every day and junk food in moderation. I have not completely given up poor habits, but I make sure to prioritize how I feel and maintain a workout schedule as well as monitoring my overall health with my doctor.

Lessons From My 20's

As a society, we must do a better job in pushing health and wellness practices and patterns early on so that we are not all being betrayed by our bodies unnecessarily too soon. Do not take good health for granted because it is not promised. I can promise you, being proactive and tending to your body's functioning ability early is always better than being reactive in any situation, but most especially with your health.

Raven Martin

Death

One of the things that come along with your brain thinking more abstractly in this phase is that you are now forced to see the world and all the things that may ensue in it through a much more complex lens. Concepts like life, death, God, purpose, pain, struggle, joy are all things that are on your radar in more complex ways than they ever really have been before. Even if you don't necessarily find yourself grappling with them personally in your 20's, when they are presented to you in the form of someone close to you dying or watching people move up in life, or you yourself move up or back in life, these sorts of concepts take on whole new meanings in your mind. I know firsthand the process of trying to understand them can become very difficult. Difficult not because you are incapable of working through it, but rather because now it is not as simple as someone telling you how and what to think any longer. Also, because you are now wrestling with the concepts while having a deeper understanding of and experience with responsibilities and duties

Lessons From My 20's

as an adult. As I said early in the book, things are just so much weightier in your 20's. One of the things that I've found that has so much more complexity and weight to it now than any other time before your 20's is death. I felt like it needed its own chapter because it is something that is completely inevitable, yet it's such a taboo subject that everyone tries to steer clear from. It's not a topic that we really force young people to discuss mostly because it is often unthinkable to imagine a young person dying. We'd consider death far too premature and completely unfair, yet it happens every day. Furthermore, the reality is that everyone is going to die, and everyone has lost someone in their lives. Whether you have yet to experience the loss of someone very close and impactful in your life, or you've loss someone as close and impactful as a biological parent, death is going to hit all our doors and there is nothing that we can do about it. To be quite honest I am still wrestling with my own thoughts about death and it's not because I am not excepting of it but rather because it is so scary to think of yourself or the people you care the most for no longer existing anymore. What I've found is that much of our fears of death are not really about death itself but rather no longer existing. All we know is this life that we are currently living and for that to suddenly cease is a very hard reality to contend with, because the question becomes, then what? No matter what happens after this life, death is something that twentysomethings should grapple with now because the way I look at it is this, your brain and all your thoughts are ripe with fresh nuance and perspective. You undoubtedly do not know it all, and you are not even close to the wisdom and perspective that you are yet to gain but, you are developing. Just like with young children around the toddler age range, between the ages of infant to five years, your minds are like a sponge during this time. With children, they are soaking in every piece of information and everything they experience. They are obviously nowhere near the level of intellect they will eventually reach, but during the time where their brains are the most impressionable, they have the capacity to soak up a wealth of information, take all of it in and develop perspective, worldview, habits, norms, morals, values and so much more. They develop their view of everything through the lens they were presented the world through. The same goes for young twentysomethings. Your brain during this time is very similar to that time of primary development, only now with much more vast capacities and abstract thinking abilities. So, for more serious and consequential concepts like death, it is important to grapple with them now while your mind can be transformed and more receptive to new thoughts, even difficult ones. As you age rigidity begins to set in and it becomes more and more difficult to develop new perceptions on complex issues. With the nature of life and adulthood being mostly complex and filled with the unexpected, I worry that so many adults are incapable of handling the inevitable aspects and nature of life. I've unfortunately witnessed so many older adults struggle with death and the loss of people close to them in ways that crippled their entire lives. Nothing can make death easy for anyone, it really is one of those things that our minds and our bodies must adjust to with time. If you see someone every day or even very often your brain creates a response system for that very person and the emotion that you get from them, and it becomes accustomed to that experience and perhaps spikes in dopamine when they are around. When that goes away your brain literally experiences emotional withdrawals similar to that of drug withdrawals that a person in rehab would go through. Without putting death into the proper context and wrestling with the philosophical truths about it in serious and mature ways, I've seen it too often destroy the trajectory of so many people's lives. This is normally the result of a person who hasn't really developed their spiritual identity and connected with theirs and all our reasons for being. Not to suggest that there is a uniformed answer and response, but what I know for certain is that death and the pain of it can be much more tolerable when you've taken the time to develop a worldview. Once you've grappled with who you are on a spiritual level and begin to maneuver through the world with a heightened level of self-awareness, death becomes an easier pill to swallow amidst the pain. When the inevitable happens like for instance, a parent or grandparent passes, this is usually the time where people begin to contend with their feelings about life and death and what they know for sure about it, if anything. I'd argue that the best time to do it is before this takes place. I know that this is also one of those subject matters where so many young adults feel as though they do not have to think about because it is so far from anything they are dealing with. The reality though, is that at any moment anyone including yourself is susceptible to death's door and how you are living and interacting with your world around you is a direct determinant of what outcomes will be left behind. This does not have to be a scary conversation or thought to have. Instead of fear and avoidance, I encourage twentysomethings to use it as a means of kickstarting the drive to begin working on the relationships with their parents, grandparents and loved ones that many so often neglect because of the fast-paced nature of this age range. Yes, you do need to be busy starting and developing a life that you can feel most proud of, but you must not neglect the things and the people that got you to where you are today. Your time will be largely consumed when you are at work putting that life together but finding a way to incorporate time with loved ones must become a priority that you build into your life during the building process. I understand fully how the realities of everyone's lives are drastically different. I know that for some, the idea of fostering a relationship with their family is not remotely ideal to say the least. That said, I always welcome every one of my clients, even those that are estranged from their families to strongly evaluate those relationships with their loved ones and what can most realistically happen within those relationships. At the end of the day, even if nothing can come of the relationships that you may have always wanted, it's always in your best interest in the long-term to get what you can from them. In the context of death and how much tomorrow is not promised, making sure that you have done all you can to connect with those that you bred from for sheer sake of blood ties and legacy is important. Even though it may not

Lessons From My 20's

always feel as though it is, I can assure you there will be parts of you later that regret the time you did not reach out or time that you lost because both parties were unwilling to make the first step. I've met so many 40 and 50-year-olds whose parents, old best friends, or close family members were on their death beds or simply inching closer to the end of their lives and they all begin the reflection process. Reflecting on how they wish they would have done things correctly in the relationship as well as in their own lives. They discuss wishing they would have been able to put their pride aside to reconcile earlier so that they could have more time to spend with one another and actually do life and not just reflect on it. At the time of writing this book, I am living in Washington DC and a local bridge just collapsed near where I live. The bridge fell on several cars, luckily no one was killed. During the same week, an apartment building in Miami randomly collapsed in the middle of the day, leaving 120 people dead and I'm sure by the time this book is released the death toll will be far worse. As I reviewed those among the dead, there were a great deal of young people, many I'm sure hadn't the slightest clue that this day would be their last. Both these instances have personified for me just how fragile life is. The moment you think you are on the high of your life incapable of coming down, the most random of incidents can take place and snatch it away from you in a moment. This is not normally the sort of things that we hear when giving advice or sharing sentiments with twentysomethings. I recognize that they are normally told that the world is their oyster and to make sure to take advantage of their youth and all that comes along with it. I have no problem with those sentiments, I just want to broaden what is thought of when these sorts of statements are made. Yes, you must seize the day and take advantage of every opportunity for fun, experiences, network, wealth, and elevation; but you must also seize the parts of your day that give you the opportunity to call you parents that you have not spoken to in a while simply because conversations are precious and not going to always be guaranteed. Reconcile that broken relationship and at least clear the air if for no other reason than to have a clear conscience, because God forbid something happens to either one of you and the regretful feelings are so steep that you're forced to learn to cope with them. No one lives forever, not even you; the sooner you realize that the better and more secure and stable your future will be. I will never advise anyone to live and love like they are going to die tomorrow, but I strongly advise everyone to do so like death is an inevitable part of life, because it is. I know many may hear that and think it is a license to be careless and if not for the life and people left behind here, I would probably think the same way. But the reality is that when we or our loved ones pass on, there are real life people here left with real life consequences both good and bad of the lives we lead. What will your affairs, your relationships, your overall environment, every place you visited, every journey you've embarked say about you? How have you been impacted? How have you impacted? Your 20's are the most opportune time to create the answer to these questions. Don't take it for granted!

Raven Martin

This book is a testament to twentysomethings everywhere! We have experienced a lot of things that are equally magnificent and terrifying, yet we continue to push every day to ensure that we are working toward self-actualization. The road isn't easy, and I hope that I've shared enough about my personal experiences for you to know that you are not alone in this journey. Remember that you have the power to direct your path now and in the future. I leave you with some rules to keep you grounded and moving forward through this extraordinary decade of life.

Lessons From My 20's

LIFE CHEAT CODES

1. Set goals both big and small and stick to them if for no other reason than to teach yourself discipline. You can always come back and revisit, but to thrive you must learn to see things through!

2. Develop relationships with older people and listen to them; you don't know everything.

3. Nurture your relationships.

4. Love yourself and others in a pure and unapologetic manner.

5. Be perpetually introspective.

6. Commit to learning and doing something new every week.

7. Don't just hate your environment or wherever you currently are in life, engage with it and make the best of it until you are in the position to do something else.

8. Live everyday with intention.

9. Don't be consumed with chaos.

10. Confront and master your traumas.

11. Experience all your feelings and make mental note of them because they'll be important later!

12. Make no excuses to forfeit responsibilities and decision making.

13. Remember time eventually dwindles, and windows of opportunity decrease.

14. Create a life that honors yourself and the legacy you want to leave behind; it does not happen overnight.

15. What do you want your life to look like? Well, get to work!

www.ingramcontent.com/pod-product-compliance
Lightning Source LLC
Chambersburg PA
CBHW060356080526
44583CB00012B/343